# ENDORSEMENTS

It has been said that in ministry, who you are counts more than what you say. This is true of Jessika Tate, the author of *The Bartimaeus Generation*. The book will impart faith, hope, and love on a journey where you find your identity and step into your destiny. The calling and cry of a generation is heard. *Jesus virus* will be contagious as you encounter Him. It is time to say yes so you can see the invisible and do the impossible! A must-read if you are hungry for more.

**Dr. Leif Hetland**
President and Founder, Global Mission Awareness
Author, *The Love Awakening*

Jessika Tate's new book, *The Bartimaeus Generation*, is a timely book, especially for those of Generation Z. Jessika focuses upon the following pertaining to Generation Z: the prophetic words over generation Z rather than any deficiencies others have given to this generation; Gen Z also is recognizing the move of the Spirit while others are missing it; Gen Z is crying out for God not to pass them by; their passionate cry of faith is bringing about a response from Heaven; Jesus is empowering Gen Z to speak boldly; Gen Z will follow Jesus when visited by Him; and the last revival at Asbury College was led by Gen Z. Jessika believes a primary responsibility of Christians at this time is to disciple this young generation.

Near the end of the book, Jessika asks questions of Gen Z that will help them realize there is more similarity than what they realize between their generations and those that precede them. One hears the passion and compassion in Jessika's heart and her resolve to be one who is committed to disciple members of Gen Z.

I have been aware of Jessika's ministry for several years. I know she entered the ministry and traveled the nations while still a teenager. She has impacted the discipleship ministry of the largest Baptist church in Brazil with 23,000 in attendance and they love her. She graduated from Global Awakening Theological Seminary with her Master's, where I learned more about her and saw her commitment to be better trained to equip others. I am grateful to have her soon join our doctoral program and believe she is great soil to sow into.

I believe this is an important book for this season, and I believe Jessika will write many more books in her lifetime. She is an amazing young leader. It has been a privilege to have had her speak at our largest conference, the Voice of the Apostles. She is a model of hope to all younger girls who one day may believe God can and will use them in ministry because of the example of Jessika Tate. I believe Jessika is to Generation Z what Heidi Baker was to the young women of the Baby Boomer, Baby Buster, and Generation X. I pray more young men and women will be touched and called through Jessika's Bartimaeus generation.

**Dr. Randy Clark**
DD, DMin, ThD, MDiv, BS Religious Studies
Overseer of the apostolic network of Global Awakening
President of Global Awakening Theological Seminar

The greatest teachings come from the union of a messenger and their message. *The Bartimaeus Generation* contains a powerful message that is the essential for such a time as this. Yet this message alone would not be nearly as impactful without the messenger. Jessika Tate is a passionate follower of Jesus who has lived this message out in the real world. As we approach what could be the greatest harvest of souls in the history of the church, we must take off the blinders of this world and embrace God's heart for the coming revival. This book will help to remove the blindness of the Church so we can restore sight to this Bartimaeus generation.

**Michael Brodeur**
Author and Consultant
PastorsCoach.com

Jessika Tate's new book, *The Bartimaeus Generation*, is a must read for every believer in preparation for a worldwide multi-generational revival. Jessika's prophetic insight and comparative analysis of Bartimaeus' ability to see the Messiah despite his blindness and Gen Z crying out "Do not pass me by," is a call to action for the church of Jesus Christ. Every reader will grasp the necessary intentionality to disciple the next generation and be captivated, motivated, and accelerated to partner with the Holy Spirit to bring unity to all generations so the great harvest of the Lord is realized.

**Reverend Joanne Moody**
Agape Freedom Fighters
Agape Equipping and Training Center
LIFE School President

*The Bartimaeus Generation* invites you to gain insight, connection, and understanding to see the Gen Z generation through the eyes of Jesus. Future revivals hinge on multi-generational collaboration, and *The Bartimaeus Generation* uncovers the gold hidden in Gen Z for us all to embrace and partner with. Jessika Tate is a seasoned leader who, through Godly revelation, invites us in on how she is currently discipling and equipping this next generation. Jessika speaks of the vision Jesus gave her to teach, empower, and enlighten us to mentor and guide our children. Heaven's future leaders will thank us as we choose to gain understanding about the Godly call on their lives. I have personally seen how Jessika has walked discipleship out—this is not a theory or a topic at a conference. Jessika has lived this discipleship model with my own children, and it has been transformational.

**Will Hart**
IRIS Global CEO

Jessika Tate carries a timely and powerful message for a generation that's desperately crying out for a real and authentic Jesus. *The Bartimaeus Generation* carries the freedom that we all crave—a freedom that only Christ can offer.

**Jacob Coyne**
StayHere Director

Jessika Tate brings an important and timely message to the Body of Christ. At a time when many have low expectations for this generation's impact on the Kingdom of God, this clarion call is to all of us to step up to the mark. This generation is like the eleventh-hour workers in the field who no one thought worthy of hire. To fulfill the Lord's massive end-time harvest, all generations are needed to work, support, train, and inspire others. The harvest is ripe, the time is now, and the workers are us! Thank you, Jessika, for amplifying the call and plan of the Lord!

**Kellie Copeland**
Kellie Copeland Ministries


*The Bartimaeus Generation* by Jessika Tate is a prophetically timely book that unveils the critical role Gen Z plays in the divine narrative of revival. With deep insights and unyielding passion, Jessika explores the biblical account of Bartimaeus and how this next generation can recognize Jesus, cast off hindrances, and be empowered by Him to speak boldly and impact the world. This book is an indispensable guide that inspires and equips the next generation to embrace their unique calling in global revival.

**Mike Signorelli**
Lead Pastor, V1 Church


Jessika Tate is a trailblazer who is carrying a fresh word and vision from Above. I was not only blessed and refreshed but challenged by this message. If you are ready to set your course for nothing less than authentic revival and awakening, start reading now!

**Jeremiah Johnson**
Best-selling author of *The Power of Consecration*
Founder of The Ark Fellowship and Altar Global

Jessika Tate is a powerful and authentic voice in our generation. Her revelation of the Bartimaeus generation will not only provoke hunger in the reader, but shift our perspective to being in a position for the greatest move of God in history. I believe that God is looking for those that will move past the critics and enter into a position of desperate pursuit. This book will help stir you to overcome fear and apathy and drive you to the point where you want Jesus and nothing else!

**Jessi Green**
Director of Saturate Global
Author of *Wildfires* and *Saturate*

# *THE* BARTIMAEUS GENERATION

DESTINY IMAGE® PUBLISHERS, INC.
P.O. Box 310, Shippensburg, PA 17257-0310
*"Publishing cutting-edge prophetic resources to supernaturally empower the body of Christ"*

This book and all other Destiny Image and Destiny Image Fiction books are available at Christian bookstores and distributors worldwide.

For more information on foreign distributors, call 717-532-3040.

Reach us on the Internet: www.destinyimage.com.

ISBN 13 TP: 9-780-7684-7689-7

ISBN 13 eBook: 9-780-7684-7690-3

For Worldwide Distribution, Printed in the USA

1 2 3 4 5 6 7 8 / 27 26 25 24 23

# *THE*
# BARTIMAEUS
# GENERATION

*Unlocking the*
*Multigenerational Secret*
*of the Coming Revival*

# JESSIKA TATE

# ACKNOWLEDGMENTS

I want to initially say thank you to every pastor/leader who has made it a priority to disciple and empower the next generation, especially to those who have opened your pulpits and your youth groups to the incredible group of young ones I lead. You are modeling multi-generational revival in the most beautiful way; thank you for paving the way even when it isn't easy. That, of course, includes the spiritual parents throughout my journey who have intentionally poured into me so that I could do the same for others. This message was birthed in part due to your investment in me.

This book would not have been possible without the help of Giulia Mynssen, who has had to hear me preach this message at least a couple hundred times over the last few years and then without complaint selflessly helped compile those thoughts into a book. There aren't enough thank-yous or ice cream cones to suffice for all your help.

Maegan Hensley who has been my best friend for two decades and conveniently has a Master's degree in English for the sole purpose of proofreading my writings, or so it seems. Thanks for always taking the time to pour over my writings.

Lastly, to Larry Sparks and the Destiny Image team. You were so kind to believe in me and this book before you ever laid eyes on the manuscript. The team went above and beyond to see this come into fruition, and I am so grateful.

# CONTENTS

## Part 2
## The Coming Revival

# INTRODUCTION

*We are required to "bet our life" that the visible world, while real, is not reality itself.*
—Dallas Willard,
*Hearing God*

If you are determined to believe every statistic you have read about this next generation then this book is not for you. However if, like me, you have read the statistics, you have sat with the improbability, you have acknowledged the challenges, and still something inside of you screams, *"With man this is impossible, but with God all things are possible"* (Matthew 19:26 NIV), then keep reading. We are entering into the greatest revival the world has ever seen.

We no longer need spiritual mothers and fathers who are hopeless. This book is written for those who look at this generation and can feel the fire in your spirit for what God wants to do. This is for those who are willing to give themselves to see God's purposes fulfilled in this generation. This is for the ones who know that

> **Statistics might be factual, but they do not tell the whole story. There is a truth that supersedes statistics.**

statistics might be factual, but they do not tell the whole story. There is a truth that supersedes statistics.

I spent the last couple of years working in a denominational church in Brazil that was overwhelmed by a Holy Spirit move. While there, I split my time predominantly between working with young people who were on fire for God and introducing denominational churches to Holy Spirit. In that time, I was reading all of the statistics while simultaneously looking at young people who were defying every negative prediction I was hearing. Oh, don't get me wrong—if you have ever worked with anyone under the age of thirty then you know how they can make you ecstatically proud one moment and then make you want to put your head through the wall in the next. (At the obviously mature age of thirty-five I am intentional about keeping this number below my own age.) I do not write this book in denial of the challenges we face. I write this book with the deep conviction that what God has in store for us, for them, is far beyond the price we will pay to disciple this generation.

Somewhere in the chaos of 2020, I heard a clear word from the Lord. The world was in upheaval, Brazil was in total lockdown, churches were closing around the globe. Where there weren't strict mandates, there was plenty of controversy. Political division was at an all-time high. Many young people I know were in the most confusing season of their lives as schools and universities went from short "vacations" to a completely online-based curriculum. It left many in the tension of what was, what will be, and the disappointing reality of what they thought would be. Every person on the planet was in some way impacted, but this young generation especially was adversely impacted as prom nights and graduations were canceled. They were boxed into rooms during what were meant to be some of the most exciting times of their young lives. Even the adult extroverts were setting up unnecessary Zoom meetings to avoid talking to the walls, until they hit Zoom fatigue and resorted to recording Tik Tok dances. I most certainly am saying that from personal experience. I posted my first ever dancing video while we were in full lockdown.

It was not shocking that we started hearing the predictions of a mental health crisis, whether it be from the reality of the difficult times or the trauma of watching older generations dancing. Topics such as anxiety, depression, suicide, and divorce became commonplace as the entire globe faced something that absolutely no one enjoys—the total loss of control of our own day-to-day lives. A wave of deconstruction came as many found themselves jaded with the church and religion while pastors tried to navigate political and racial upheaval. While every message I was hearing was negative, even from the pulpit, God's voice came. As He always does, He brought a different perspective. As clear as I have ever heard Him, He declared loudly in my spirit:

*"This is a Bartimaeus generation!"*

As much as I wanted to reply with a faith filled "yes" in return, I'll be honest I did not have a clue what He meant by that. What is a

Bartimaeus generation? I could not help but notice that He did not say a "Blind Bartimaeus" generation. Admittedly, that would have been right in line with what most people think of this next generation. They are blind! No, instead He called them a Bartimaeus generation. As per usual, when He spoke, there was an infusion of hope attached. A hope that I knew the world was lacking. A hope that even the body of Christ was missing. I may not have had one single clue as to what He meant, but I was determined to find out. Journey with me as we discover what God has to say about this generation—this Bartimaeus generation!

*PART 1*

## SEEING GEN Z THROUGH THE STORY OF BLIND BARTIMAEUS

*Chapter 1*

# THE BARTIMAEUS GENERATION

*Our rebellion against God, even as believers,*
*is fueled by the toxic fumes of unbelief.*
—James MacDonald,
*Christ-Centered Biblical Counseling*

If you pick up a book called *The Bartimaeus Generation*, then I make some automatic assumptions about you. Apologies in advance if these are incorrect; we all know what assumptions do. One thing I assume is that you have a relationship with Jesus. The next thing I assume is that you have some sort of interest in this generation. Perhaps you are a pastor, a parent, a grandparent, a researcher, a theologian, or simply an interested leader. If not one of those two, then maybe you thought this was a fiction story. Either way, I am excited for you to take this journey with me. I am hungry for revival in my lifetime. I live to see God's Spirit poured out. I meet people all the time who say they want revival, but who have become so familiar with what the news says that they do not actually have any faith for it.

As a believer I have learned that God sees things differently than the world does. If we are honest, He often sees things differently than we do. Let me give you some examples. I see a trial and can think of a million reasons to complain, but God sees a trial and has a million reasons to rejoice (James 1:2). God sees the Red Sea and envisions a dry bridge to safety. Only God watches His servants being thrown into a fiery furnace and somehow thinks it would make the story more interesting if they turn the heat up even hotter. He then displays His power and protection when the men walk out not even smelling like smoke (Daniel 3:27).

He is undoubtedly the God who is in these tiny details, and yet He sure loves to show up in big, undeniable ways too. No wonder Elijah decided that calling down fire from Heaven wasn't enough—why not throw some water on the wood to liven things up a bit (1 Kings 18:33)? When humans meet impossibilities, God starts preparing for testimonies. This is indeed the God who loves to do the impossible. He loves to challenge our ways of thinking and ultimately prove that He is God, the all-powerful One who has never met a situation that caused Him to be afraid. He is the God of victory who literally laughs at the futile attempts of the enemy (Psalm 2:4).

So why then do so many Christians start recounting the statistics instead of the prophecies when they are discussing this generation? Why is it that we do not only hear the negative report from the media, but also from the pulpit? By the way, I have regrettably been guilty of this too. You might see this generation dead like Lazarus, but I think God sees a resurrection story that defies all odds and sets a generation free. He is not intimidated by the mental health crisis. He has yet to be confused by our challenges. Not one time has the Father turned to Jesus and said, "I am just not sure what We are going to do."

When it comes to this generation, I have somewhat of a unique perspective. I spent the last couple of years living in Brazil surrounded by young people who silence all of the critics. I have watched children heal the sick, prophesy, and cast out demons. I have traveled with young women ministers who know how to usher Holy Spirit into a room and partner with Him to see signs, miracles, and wonders. I went to an active war zone in the Ukraine with an eighteen- and twenty-year-old who bravely went where others were too afraid to go to share the Gospel and selflessly love the hurting. While we were there, not only did I have my two fearless young ones, but we were also met by crews of young people who boldly preached the Gospel with power.

I have seen far too much to be pessimistic. After countless miracles, signs, wonders, and transformations, you cannot convince me that this generation is a lost cause. There is an aspect of personal experience that has the ability to shift perspective. I am telling you upfront that I have an agenda with this book. I have no intention of having an ulterior motive; I want to make it plain and clear for you. I want to shift your perspective. I want to influence what you think about this generation. I want you to believe for the impossible with me. More importantly, I want you to believe what He has said with me. Then, I want all of us to work together for the revival that is coming.

In the middle of the pandemic I found myself longing for the church to realize just what God wanted to do in this generation. I was frustrated with the consistent chatter I heard about how this generation is "this" or "that" and is basically a hopeless cause. It seemed like everywhere I turned, from watching a news story to listening to a sermon, there was another statistic that condemned this generation as a lost cause to a burgeoning mental health crisis. Don't misunderstand me; I have read the statistics. In fact, I am very familiar with them. I have read the studies and spent countless hours mentoring young people in the midst of their generational struggles. I have sat with the facts and even felt the hopelessness too. There were times I felt like I was drowning in the ocean of impossibility. It was in this season that God spoke to me one day so very clearly:

**After countless miracles, signs, wonders, and transformations, you cannot convince me that this generation is a lost cause.**

*"This is a Bartimaeus generation!"*

I absolutely love when God speaks. There is nothing else that awakens my soul like His voice; however, this particular time I had absolutely no idea what He meant. Little did I know that in the coming months I would spend much of my time seeking God for the significance of His statement. It led to countless hours studying Bartimaeus' story in the Bible. I came to know Bartimaeus so well that it almost feels like when I get to Heaven he might be one of my best friends there. I often refer to Bartimaeus as Barti or, more affectionately, my "spiritual boyfriend." I have found in Barti a hope that defies logic for this generation and this next move of God that is coming. While many have felt the defeatism of the statistics, I have a fire of hope rising up from within me. Despite what you might have heard or read about this generation, there is a Bartimaeus anointing on them and they will be a generation that sees revival. I am not ignoring the facts, I am just trusting the truth that comes from a higher voice. He speaks a better word. There is no truth apart from Him, in spite of what the world might tell you.

Let's take a minute to look at the story of Blind Bartimaeus in the Gospel of Mark for those of you haven't yet become as intimately familiar with him as I have. There is no pressure to have a spiritual crush on Barti like I do; however, I have no doubt that as you spend a little more time with him, he will inspire you just as he has me. Throughout this book, we are going to dive into this story on a deeper level and unveil God's words over this generation.

## THE STORY OF BLIND BARTIMAEUS

*Then they came to Jericho. As Jesus and his disciples, together with a large crowd, were leaving the city, a blind man, Bartimaeus (which means "son of Timaeus"), was sitting by the roadside begging. When he heard that it was Jesus of Nazareth, he began to shout, "Jesus, Son of David, have mercy on me!"*

*Many rebuked him and told him to be quiet, but he shouted all the more, "Son of David, have mercy on me!"*

*Jesus stopped and said, "Call him."*

*So they called to the blind man, "Cheer up! On your feet! He's calling you." Throwing his cloak aside, he jumped to his feet and came to Jesus.*

*"What do you want me to do for you?" Jesus asked him.*

*The blind man said, "Rabbi, I want to see."*

*"Go," said Jesus, "your faith has healed you." Immediately he received his sight and followed Jesus along the road* (**Mark 10:46-52 NIV**).

We enter the story of Blind Bartimaeus as Jesus makes a seemingly unplanned stop in Jericho on His way to Jerusalem. As the text notes, Jesus arrives in Jericho with a "large crowd." This is not surprising as Jesus often drew large crowds everywhere He went. There were many who were following Jesus and watching as Jesus went about destroying the works of darkness (1 John 3:8). Jesus was healing the sick, casting out demons, and turning the current religious system upside down. What an exciting time to be in the region where Jesus was walking. In addition to the crowd that would typically follow Jesus as He went on mission from city to city, there were likely even more on the road He was taking. We know that Passover was coming soon and many would be on their way, taking a pilgrimage to Jerusalem to celebrate, just as Jesus was.

Bartimaeus' story has much to teach us about Jesus, the nature of the Kingdom of God, and I believe about what God is doing in this current generation. Together we are going to explore the richness of God's Word and how He so lovingly uses His Word to reveal to us His plans and purposes.

## PRAYER

As we launch into these next chapters, let's take a minute to stop and pray. Would you join me?

> Father, I pray that You would pour out Your Holy Spirit right now on whoever is reading these words. Give us both the gift of seeing You rightly and seeing others rightly. Will You help us to lay aside our previous notions and ideas of You, of ourselves, and of this generation? As we venture into this book together, help us to renew our minds with the truth of what You have to say about this generation. Lord, we believe what *You* say about them; help our unbelief, help our doubts, give us grace. Forgive us for the times that we have limited You due to what we have seen with our eyes. Give us Your eyes to see. Pour out Your Spirit on this generation and encounter them with Your radical,

transforming love. Raise up leaders who would lead in character and power. We love You, Lord; we trust You, Lord. Send revival to us. Revive us, revive our churches, revive our cities, revive our nation. All for Your glory, in Jesus' name, amen.

# REFLECTION QUESTIONS

1. What messages and opinions have you heard about the upcoming generation?

2. What type of feeling have you held in the past about the upcoming generation?

3. What seems to you like the biggest "impossibility" plaguing the upcoming generation?

4. Can you think of a person in the Bible whom God changed radically? Are today's challenges any harder for God?

5. Have you personally witnessed Kingdom potential in young people?

6. As you prayed the prayer, what did God show you about His dreams for today's youth?

# Chapter 2

# LIVING BEYOND LIMITATIONS

*We are all, at times, unconscious prophets.*
—Charles Spurgeon, *The Salt-Cellars*

*Then they came to Jericho. As Jesus and his disciples, together with a large crowd, were leaving the city, a blind man, Bartimaeus (which means "son of Timaeus"), was sitting by the roadside begging.*
—Mark 10:46 NIV

One of the first things we must take note of in the story of blind Bartimaeus is that he is blind. It sounds so menial, doesn't it? We will come to find that this blind man saw better than most.

This man we are going to come to know was more known for his current condition than for anything else about him. The culture of today continues to repeat the pattern of identifying others by their lack. So often we fail to recognize anything else about a

**The culture of today continues to repeat the pattern of identifying others by their lack.**

person besides their disability, their failure, their weaknesses. Bartimaeus faced this challenge as well. Bartimaeus as a blind beggar is on the fringe of society and lives at the mercy of others to provide for him. He is at this time completely dependent on those who would pass by him. It is actually quite remarkable that Mark even takes the time to mention his name. Most of the names of the recipients of miracles are omitted in the Gospels. Bartimaeus' name does not have some deep, hidden meaning that would cause his name to be notable; it simply means "son of Timaeus."[1] There is absolutely nothing about Bartimaeus in the eyes of society that would even make him worth mentioning; however, Jesus must have found something in Bartimaeus worth stopping for, worth mentioning, worth our attention.

There are many of these stories in the Bible. God takes the unlikely and the forgotten. He takes the one that most would never pick. I grew up playing sports, and to this day I have a competitive edge in my nature. I spent many summers as a kid playing games like kickball where before every game we would line up and start the process of picking teams. Team captains would scan the available players and look for specific attributes that would make them an ideal teammate. We would look for speed, agility, and power. It was not complicated to know which characteristics you were looking for in a talented athlete. Everyone would know which kids would be chosen first because we all wanted the best players on our team. Inevitably, the last kids picked were those who, put as politely as I can, just were not fierce competitors.

When we look throughout the Bible though, God appears to pick the ones without qualifications. If anything, He chooses the ones with severe disqualifications. God seems to have different eligibility requirements than we do. I would not pick a murderer to write the majority of the New Testament (Apostle Paul) and yet God does. My best assumption is that God must see what we often cannot.

One of my heroes is a lady named Corrie ten Boom. Corrie's story is a remarkable testimony of how God can use anyone, regardless of their qualifications. In the midst of World War II, Corrie and her family risked their lives to hide Jews from the Nazis in their home in the Netherlands. Despite being an unlikely hero, Corrie saw God's hand at work in her life and willingly obeyed His call to help those in need. She later wrote about her experiences in *The Hiding Place*, which has inspired countless readers around the world. As if that wasn't enough, beyond saving the lives of many during World War II, Corrie went on to travel the globe preaching on forgiveness after her experiences in the Nazi concentration camps.

> **I would not pick a murderer to write the majority of the New Testament (Apostle Paul) and yet God does.**

This woman had no formal training or background that would qualify her for all that she did in her lifetime. She was just a simple, single woman whom God chose to use to do the extraordinary. Her story reminds me that God chooses the improbable. He habitually disregards outward appearances and overt talents. Corrie knew that she was not the most qualified candidate to be used so mightily of God and encourages us with this statement, "It is not my ability, but my response to God's ability, that counts."

This generation has become known by their weaknesses. The body of Christ echoes the concerns of society by treating Gen Z as a diseased leper or one plagued by disability that cannot be overcome. They have been labeled with all sorts of names, including "the new lost generation." For so many reasons, they feel like the ones we cannot connect with. The church has experienced much of the same, hosting entire conferences focused solely on how we recapture a generation that has been lost.

The problem with this is that believers were never meant to simply accept the narrative of society or culture. Christians are meant to be thermostats, not thermometers. Your job is not to tell the world what the temperature in the room is. Honestly, anyone can do that. When I walk outside my home in the Tennessee summer it does not take a prophet to tell me that it is hot and humid! There are plenty of dramatic effects of the temperature. The outpouring of sweat, the horrific clinging of your clothes to every unpolished part of your body—absolutely everyone can see and feel the devastatingly hot temperature. As a Christian your job is not to tell what the temperature in the room is, your job is to set the temperature in the room. Be a thermostat, not a thermometer. Christians have a unique purpose. I would even say a unique privilege. In Ezekiel 37 we have a fascinating story.

> *The hand of the Lord was on me, and he brought me out by the Spirit of the Lord and set me in the middle of a valley; it was full of bones. He led me back and forth among them, and I saw a great many bones on the floor of the valley, bones that were very dry. He asked me, "Son of man, can these bones live?"*
>
> *I said, "Sovereign Lord, you alone know."*
>
> *Then he said to me, "Prophesy to these bones and say to them, 'Dry bones, hear the word of the Lord! This is what the Sovereign Lord says to these bones: I will make breath enter you, and you will come to life. I will attach tendons to you and make flesh come upon you and cover you with skin; I will put breath in you, and you will come to life. Then you will know that I am the Lord.'"*
>
> *So I prophesied as I was commanded. And as I was prophesying, there was a noise, a rattling sound, and the bones came together, bone to bone. I looked, and tendons and flesh appeared on them and skin covered them, but there was no breath in them.*
>
> *Then he said to me, "Prophesy to the breath; prophesy, son of man, and say to it, 'This is what the Sovereign Lord says: Come, breath, from the four winds and breathe into these slain, that they may live.'" So I prophesied as*

*he commanded me, and breath entered them; they came to life and stood up on their feet—a vast army.*

*Then he said to me: "Son of man, these bones are the people of Israel. They say, 'Our bones are dried up and our hope is gone; we are cut off.' Therefore prophesy and say to them: 'This is what the Sovereign Lord says: My people, I am going to open your graves and bring you up from them; I will bring you back to the land of Israel. Then you, my people, will know that I am the Lord, when I open your graves and bring you up from them. I will put my Spirit in you and you will live, and I will settle you in your own land. Then you will know that I the Lord have spoken, and I have done it, declares the Lord'"* (**Ezekiel 37:1-14 NIV**).

God asks Ezekiel a question. It would be natural for Ezekiel to respond with a confident, *"Absolutely not!"* Dry bones cannot live again—or can they? Again, it does not take a prophet or even any measure of spirituality to know that dry bones are quite far from living. Having read this story many times, it is hard to imagine Ezekiel explaining to God exactly why bones cannot live. It seems inconceivable that there in this moment with God present he would take the time to explain to God how life actually works. The reality is that bones have no life inside of them to live. They require more to function—primarily, they require breath. Perhaps Ezekiel could spout off a biology lesson to ensure that God knew it was indeed impossible for dry bones to live. I mean, if we are being honest with ourselves, isn't this what we do?

God asks if a nation can be saved, and we explain to Him how secular the nation is. Usually, we have a few questions of our own. "Well, God, have You seen the abortion rate? Of course this nation cannot be saved!" God asks if a body can be healed, and we show Him the doctor's diagnosis. He challenges us, asking if our loved ones could serve God, and we recount the depth of the sin they are in as if He was unaware. He asks us if a young generation can bring revival and we start discussing the suicide rates. There's a reason that God told the prophet Isaiah, *"My thoughts are not your thoughts"* (Isaiah 55:8 NIV). Is this how God intends it? His army of believers reciting the latest news story? In my own personal life I have found that if I don't know what God has to say about it then maybe it is best if I just keep my mouth shut. *"Even a fool who keeps silent is considered wise; when he closes his lips, he is deemed intelligent"* (Proverbs 17:28 ESV).

When God asks Ezekiel if the bones can live, he actually responds with one of the wisest responses we see throughout the entire Bible: *"O Lord God, you know"* (Ezekiel 37:3 ESV). Let his answer be a lesson for us. Next time God asks us a question, maybe we shouldn't bother telling God what He already knows. Maybe we should ask Him what He knows that we obviously don't. At least, not yet.

> If I don't know what God has to say about it then maybe it is best if I just keep my mouth shut.

How shocking that God's answer to Ezekiel was not rebuke for refusing to answer His question. Rather, God gave a truth that was stronger than reality. The reality is dry bones cannot live unless the Creator says they can. What is important in this story and in our story is not what the current conditions are; rather, it is what God is saying. Your greatest weapon against the enemy is knowing what God says about you and your situation. Beyond just knowing what He says is discovering what He is telling us to say. God does not just tell Ezekiel the bones can live and then they come to life. God actually tells Ezekiel to prophesy to the bones himself! As we read, Ezekiel prophesies into those bones and the impossible happens. Muscles begin to grow; ligaments, veins, and a body begin to form. Eventually, God tells him to prophesy breath, and then the breath of life enters the bodies and everything changes.

**Your greatest weapon against the enemy is knowing what God says about you and your situation.**

Where humans saw dry bones, God saw an army.

The Bible tells us that *"life and death are in the power of the tongue"* (Proverbs 18:21 HCSB). There's two main problems when believers continually quote the statistics about this generation. First, you were never meant to be a thermometer. You were supposed to be a thermostat. Second, life and death is in our tongue. As we repeat negativity and death over this generation, we are cursing them with our mouths. Our job is to bless them, not to curse them. Consider Proverbs 11:25 (ESV) next time before you start cursing this generation or anyone for that matter: *"Whoever brings blessing will be enriched, and one who waters will himself be watered."*

Listen, reader. New friend. Take the time to hear what God is saying about this generation. Press in to hear what He is saying about your circumstances. It is so easy to parrot what you can see with your natural eyes. Perhaps you have areas of your life, your church, your city, your job where all you see is dead bones. It looks by all evidence to be dead. In fact, maybe the reality is that it is dead, but there is a truth that is so much bigger than reality. What is God saying? What does God see? If God sees an army, I do not want to waste my time talking and complaining about dry bones.

One more Bible illustration to hit this point home. In 2 Kings 6 we find such a powerful story. Elisha the prophet had greatly angered the king of Syria by consistently revealing the king's battle plans to his opponent, the king of Israel, every time the king of Syria would try to attack. In response, the king of Syria had sent an entire army to kill Elisha, and that is where we pick up in the story.

> *So he sent there horses and chariots and a great army, and they came by night and surrounded the city. When the servant of the man of God rose early in the morning and went out, behold, an army with horses and chariots was all around the city. And the servant said, "Alas, my master! What shall we do?" He said, "Do not be afraid, for those who are with us are more than those who are with them." Then Elisha prayed and said, "O Lord, please open his eyes that he may see." So the Lord opened the eyes of the young man, and he saw, and behold,*

*the mountain was full of horses and chariots of fire all around Elisha* (**2 Kings 6:14-17 ESV**).

At first, Elisha's servant could only see with his natural eyes. He saw the very real army that surrounded them and was understandably afraid. In spite of that, Elisha saw what his servant did not. Elisha saw what was true in the spirit. Seeing in the spirit does not deny what is real in front of us; it discerns and acknowledges the reality of the spirit. Elisha saw the angelic armies that were present for his defense. He prayed simply for his servant, "O Lord, please open his eyes that he may see."

Let me ask you some questions.

"Dear friend, can this generation possibly be the greatest harvesters the world has ever seen?"

"Is it possible that Gen Z will pioneer the next move of God?"

"Can Gen Z set the captives free of anxiety, depression, and suicide?"

**Seeing in the spirit does not deny what is real in front of us; it discerns and acknowledges the reality of the spirit.**

"What if there is more to be seen than what our natural eyes tell us?"

Finally, "Would you rather be a thermometer or a thermostat in this end-time revival?"

## PRAYER

Take a moment right now and sit with Holy Spirit.

Ask Him, "Holy Spirit, what are the lies that I have believed about this generation or even specific young men and women in this generation?"

As He speaks to you, write down what He shows you.

Then ask Him, "Holy Spirit what do You say about this generation? What do You say about this specific person?"

Once you have heard what He says, pray with me. Your prayers are powerful. Pray over the specific young people you know or Holy Spirit is highlighting.

> Lord, we lift this generation up to You. We repent for believing the lies of the enemy. We repent for echoing word curses, and we ask that You break off the curses spoken over this generation. We believe Your blood speaks a better word. We believe that what You say is more important than what anyone else says. We believe that Your words are more important than what we see and feel with our own eyes. Give us eyes to see the army in the midst of the dry bones. Heal this generation. Breathe life into them. Raise up Your army of young warriors, all for Your glory. In Jesus' name, amen.

## Note

1. Craig S. Keener, *The IVP Bible Background Commentary: New Testament* (Downers Grove, IL: InterVarsity Press, 2014), 155.

# REFLECTION QUESTIONS

1. What limitations have you seen in Gen Z?

2. In what ways have you participated in limiting young people through your words or expectations of them?

3. How is God calling you to participate in breaking off these limits and curses?

4. Do you need to repent for your attitude toward any young person or Gen Z as a whole?

5. What vision did God show you for Gen Z when praying?

6. Who is God highlighting to you as a young person He wants you to bless?

# Chapter 3

# RECOGNIZING JESUS WHEN NO ONE ELSE DOES

*Being willing to do what you are not qualified
to do is sometimes what qualifies you.*

—Bill Johnson

*When he heard that it was Jesus of Nazareth, he began
to shout, "Jesus, Son of David, have mercy on me!"*

—Mark 10:47 NIV

As Jesus walked the earth in flesh, many people never recognized Him as Messiah. Theologians often call this the "Messianic secret"—the challenging reality that even as Jesus stood right in front of their face, they had no idea who He really was. Repeatedly Jesus was misjudged, even so far as being accused of being a demon Himself (Matthew 12:24).

In spite of all of those who did not recognize Jesus, Bartimaeus did. It seems paradoxical that a blind man could recognize anyone, much less recognize the One whom so many, especially the most religious in society, did not. Again, Bartimaeus was blind. Bartimaeus was a beggar. Bartimaeus was not a prophet. He was not yet a disciple. He was a blind beggar. As already stated, he had no social status or qualifications that would make him in any way notable. As far as we know, he had no previous experiences or encounters with Jesus. In every way Bartimaeus was one discounted and overlooked by society. He was essentially unqualified for the revelation that he carried.

Isn't it quite ironic, then, that it was him, a blind beggar, who actually recognized Jesus not just as a Healer, but as Messiah? As a beggar, Bartimaeus would be seated on a well-traveled road in order to have more opportunity for charity. As people traveled by, it is likely that Bartimaeus could hear the discussions of passersby. He quite possibly heard some of the miracle stories. There is a good chance he even heard of Jesus giving sight to another blind man (Mark 8:22-25). This blind man was healed in Bethsaida, about ninety-four miles from Jericho. I can imagine that the story was being passed from city to city. At some point someone would stop to tell this blind beggar of this Man who had healed another blind man. Can you imagine Bartimaeus hearing these stories? What might he feel when he hears that there is One who can heal the blind? Radical hope might arise, hoping that one day this Man might just pass his way.

In addition to hearing the stories, he would have heard some of the rumors of who people thought Jesus was (Mark 8:28). I am sure he heard the gossip and the critics as well. Somewhere in all of it, a faith and expectation came into Bartimaeus.

Then one day, Bartimaeus' time comes. He hears the crowds coming. The constant chatter about Jesus. Could this be Him? Is the One he had heard the stories about making His way toward him? Bartimaeus has spent days pondering how he will respond if Jesus ever comes near him. He has believed in his heart that this is Him. This is the Messiah. He has hoped, he has prayed for this very moment. How will he respond?

I imagine all of his faith, his hope, even his desperation overwhelms him in this moment and all he can do is shout at the top of his lungs. "Jesus, Son of David, have mercy on me!"

Despite all the mixed commentary Bartimaeus hears about Jesus, he knows deep down who He is, and when the moment comes, he chooses one distinct phrase to refer to Him. A phrase that is not used at any other point in the Gospel of Mark. Bartimaeus calls Jesus the "Son of David." This phrase is a Messianic term, which means that Bartimaeus recognizes Jesus as the Savior, as the long awaited Messiah, the One who was to come and set His people free.

Bartimaeus recognized Him *before* he was healed of his own physical blindness. Before Bartimaeus "saw" a miracle, he saw who Jesus was. R.T. France reminds us that, "no other onlooker has interpreted Jesus in Messianic terms...in this Gospel."[1] Bartimaeus was only the second in Mark's Gospel to even recognize Jesus as Messiah, and the first was Peter, a close disciple who knew Jesus well. The setting for Bartimaeus' acknowledgment of Jesus comes not long after a little excerpt where Jesus asks the disciples who they think He is in Mark 8:27-29 (ESV).

> *And Jesus went on with his disciples to the villages of Caesarea Philippi. And on the way he asked his disciples, "Who do people say that I am?" And they told him, "John the Baptist; and others say, Elijah; and others, one of the prophets." And he asked them, "But who do you say that I am?" Peter answered him, "You are the Christ."*

Peter wisely answers "You are the Christ" in verse 29, becoming the first one other than demons to declare Him as Messiah. In this passage, again we feel the tension of the Messianic secret. Though many walked with Him, they did not recognize Him.

It is absolutely remarkable that a blind beggar could identify Jesus before the theologically trained, before the priests, the pharisees, perhaps even those who had been following Jesus. This seems to be a continual problem throughout the history of humankind. There are many who are more focused on rules and religious formulas than on who Jesus is. These who have been oversaturated in knowledge typically have a much more difficult time recognizing Jesus, the Messiah, when He shows up.

Bartimaeus teaches us that spiritual sight is way more beneficial than physical sight. As Jesus says to Thomas in John 20:29 (NASB), *"Because you have seen Me, have you now believed? Blessed are they who did not see, and yet believed."* Bartimaeus is one of those. He may not have seen Jesus with his physical eyes, but he saw Him in the Spirit. He saw Him for who He really was.

While I was working on my Master's degree in seminary, I often heard the familiar jokes about theological education. "It's not seminary, it's cemetery," or even, "Seminary is where faith goes to die!" Thankfully

## It is not head knowledge that produces intimacy.

this was not my experience at all, but there is a reality that it is not head knowledge that enables us to recognize Him. It is not head knowledge that produces intimacy. In fact, many times what we think we know can deeply hinder us from greater revelation. I am all for theological training and learning all that we possibly can about the Word of God; however, that is not to be confused with actually *knowing Him*. Knowing about Him and knowing Him are two completely different things. The tragedy is just as we see in the Gospels—when knowing about the law, knowing about the Scriptures, knowing about God does not produce a hunger inside of us to actually know Him, we easily become judgmental toward those who are seeking Him purely. Theologians are often the harshest critics of revival and outpourings. Instead of acknowledging the God of revival encountering and reviving His people, many often choose to attempt to discredit or even disprove what He is doing.

Likewise, there can be those who have known Jesus; who have spent time with Him; who have watched Him move, heal, deliver; who have been part of major revivals in the past, and yet when He comes again they don't recognize Him. Their previous knowledge hinders their current revelation. I remember hearing Pastor Bill

Johnson say one time that the greatest hindrance to the next move of God is often those who were part of the last move of God.

Bartimaeus was in all certainty theologically unqualified, but perhaps that is exactly what qualified him. He had absolutely nothing to lean on except the belief that this was indeed Jesus.

This generation is one that has been discredited. They have been looked down upon. We have labeled them as spiritually blind, immature, and essentially unqualified. They are the ones the church has looked at as a lost generation. We have been concerned with how to reach them while God was planning ways for them to lead us. I am not criticizing our attempts to draw them in. In fact, I applaud those who prayed and sought wisdom for how to reach this next generation. What I am saying is that as God began to raise them up as leaders, we all became quite uncomfortable with it. Perhaps we wanted them to come follow us, but we were far unprepared to follow them. Isn't this how it often goes in our lives? We pray for God to move. We pray for God to touch a generation. We pray that God would send revival, and then when it comes we are quite bothered with the way He chose to do it.

As young people began to worship for hours and hours, the critics came out of the woodwork. Many were bothered by how imperfect it was, some critical because the Gospel wasn't preached enough, others upset because of how they responded to the Gospel. As Jesus became present, this generation recognized Him and they responded.

They recognized Him.

These young people whom many deemed as lost were the first ones to truly pick up on what God was doing in their generation. They did not stop and wait for a theologian's interpretation. They did not wait to see if their response would be acceptable. They were not the ones posting all over social media and trying to get fame. They just responded to His Presence.

> **It was unpolished and unproduced. It was an honest prayer.**

When Bartimaeus recognized who was coming his direction, he began to cry out. You see, Bartimaeus was determined that if Jesus was anywhere in the vicinity he must get His attention. He had decided that if Jesus was indeed the Messiah then he could not sit idly by. Bartimaeus decided right then and there that he would do whatever was necessary for Jesus to come near to him. It was unpolished and unproduced. It was an honest prayer.

C.H. Spurgeon describes the cry of Bartimaeus in one of his sermons:

> That is prayer, when the poor soul in some weighty trouble, fainting and athirst, lifts up its streaming eyes, and wrings its hands, and beats its bosom, and then cries, "Thou Son of David, have mercy on me." Your cold orations will ne'er reach the throne of God. It is the burning lava of the soul that hath a furnace within—a very volcano of grief and sorrow—it is that burning lava of prayer that finds its way to God. No

prayer ever reaches God's heart which does not come from our hearts. Nine out of ten of the prayers which ye listen to in our public services have so little zeal in them, that if they obtained a blessing it would be a miracle of miracles indeed.[2]

> It will not go well on an mp3 recording, and it certainly isn't good marketing. It is earnest zeal for the Lord coming out in a cry from this generation.

As this generation began to recognize the real Jesus, they cried out. As moves of God are popping up all around the world, this generation cries out to Jesus. The hunger in their heart says that if God is going to move in their generation then they will not sit back and watch while He moves in other places through other people. They have read the stories of the past revivals and decided that they do not want to spend their lives telling stories of past revivals; they want to live one. This cry has rung out across the nations. The cry of a generation that says, "God, if You are pouring out Your Spirit then pour it out here. Pour it out in me." It is not pretty. It is not rehearsed. It is unrefined. It will not go well on an mp3 recording, and it certainly isn't good marketing. It is earnest zeal for the Lord coming out in a cry from this generation. Instead of criticizing and picking it apart, we should probably join in.

## PRAYER

Let me pray for this same cry of hunger to rise up inside of you. After you read this prayer, would you set this book down and pray yourself. Let the cry of holy hunger rise up inside of your heart.

> Father, I pray for those reading this book right now that a hunger is being birthed inside of their heart. Holy Spirit, in this moment would You overwhelm them wherever they are. Would You produce a hunger so strong inside of them that they refuse to be satisfied with anything less than a full manifestation of Your Presence. Do in us what You did in Bartimaeus that day. Let the realization of who You are transform us. Jesus Christ. Our Messiah. Our coming King. Lord of lords and King of kings. Alpha and Omega. We want nothing but You. Take away all of the temporary things that try to steal our affection and attention. We want You, Jesus. Amen.

Notes

1. R.T. France, *The Gospel of Mark,* The New International Greek Testament Commentary (Eerdmans, 2002), 423.

2. C.H. Spurgeon, "The Blind Beggar," sermon no. 266, August 7, 1859.

# REFLECTION QUESTIONS

1. What contexts are most comfortable or familiar for you to experience God's Presence?

2. Have you ever encountered Jesus' Presence in a way that surprised you or caught you off guard?

3. Does Jesus have ways of showing up that you would not immediately recognize as Him?

4. How can you prepare your heart to soften and welcome Him if He does show up in a way that seems strange to you?

5. As you prayed, how did you feel your hunger for His Presence increasing?

6. Are there any other people, especially young people, you might need to become more vulnerable with in order to catch each other's hunger for more of God?

*Chapter 4*

# IGNORE THE CRITICS

*When he heard that it was Jesus of Nazareth, he began to shout, "Jesus, Son of David, have mercy on me!" Many rebuked him and told him to be quiet, but he shouted all the more, "Son of David, have mercy on me!"*
—Mark 10:47-48 NIV

*Don't be distracted by criticism. Remember, the only taste of success some people have is when they take a bite out of you.*
—Zig Ziglar

After Bartimaeus initially cried out in faith to Jesus, those around him responded by rebuking him. These people were likely in the crowd that was following with Jesus. You would think that these would be the ones who would encourage Bartimaeus. The hope would be that the people around Bartimaeus and especially the people around Jesus would be the ones rooting for him! Cheering him on to get his miracle. Is that not what we are asked to do as fellow believers? I do not want to be the one who attempts to quiet the faith of others, but rather the one who throws gasoline on their fire. As 1 Thessalonians 5:11 (NIV) says, *"Therefore encourage one another and build each other up."*

We see a perfect example of this in Mark 2:1-5 when Jesus healed a man who was a paralytic. It was not just any ordinary miracle (not that any miracle is ordinary). In this story, it was the man's friends who did anything possible to make sure Jesus paid attention to the paralytic. Most of you are familiar with the story. Jesus had been doing miracles, setting captives free, and ultimately utterly destroying the works of the enemy. Word had been circulating, and when Jesus came near, these four friends decided there was no way they could let this opportunity go to waste. If Jesus was in the vicinity, they decided they would make sure that He healed their friend. The Bible says that when Jesus saw the faith of the friends, He healed the paralytic. It was literally the faith of the friends that brought Jesus' attention to the paralytic. Notice the difference between the friends of the paralytic and the people surrounding Bartimaeus. One group was beyond willing to support their friend, doing everything possible to help, and the other group was doing anything they could to hinder Bartimaeus' faith.

We do a fairly good job in youth ministry emphasizing the importance of the people we are connected to, but we often neglect this when ministering to adults. Let me tell you that regardless of your age, gender, race, denomination, or aspirations, whom you surround yourself with matters. Your community is either pushing you toward Jesus or hindering you from Him. They are either supporting your goals or they are distracting you from them.

Let us return to the text of Bartimaeus. When I read the Bible I love to imagine myself in the story. What was being said? What was the atmosphere like? I call these imaginations the JTV or Jessika Tate Version. Journey with me for a minute into the JTV, or my speculation of what might have occurred. (Disclaimer: I am in no way trying to add to Scripture or claiming this is exactly what happened, I am simply trying to add a potential perspective.)

Bartimaeus is sitting out on a sunny day in the pitch darkness. His heightened sense of hearing means he is hearing the whispers of the crowd. Then he starts to hear the noises of a large group coming toward him on their journey to Jerusalem. The name of Jesus undoubtedly is mentioned repeatedly. With no way to verify with his own eyes if it is Jesus, the One he has heard the stories about, he resorts to unashamed shouting, pleas for mercy.

His screaming and idiotic behavior quickly incurs a harsh reaction from the crowd. I imagine that immediately multiple rebukes are aimed at Bartimaeus.

"You are being *too* loud!"

"Don't bother Him, do you *know* who He is!"

"Could you just calm down?"

"He is not going to stop for someone like you!"

"If He wanted to talk to you then He would come to you!"

The collective "shhhhhhh" of the masses rings out. In the midst of this group walking with Jesus, why would this one man make the prideful assumption that the Master would stop for him? Especially for him, a nobody blind beggar.

## Extreme passion is often offensive to the apathetic.

I'm sure the crowd rebuking him knew all the reasons why it was best that Bartimaeus keep quiet. I'm sure they had all their ideas about what Jesus would think about his excessive screaming. There is no doubt that everyone had their opinions. They had their opinions about Bartimaeus and they had their opinions about Jesus. Just as Mary with that alabaster jar had found a love and intimacy that compelled her to pour out such a costly offering. Jesus took that woman with the alabaster jar, and as the religious criticized her actions, He decided to memorialize her offering forever (Matthew 26:13). What the religious thought was excessive, Jesus found great delight in.

I can resonate with this scenario. What I have found is that extreme passion is often offensive to the apathetic. It is the extremely religious who lean toward anger when others break out of the boxes we prefer they stay in. We do not mind passion unless it challenges our lack of it. It is okay for you to be a little loud, just do not be louder than everyone else. It is fine if you feel the need to raise your hands a little, just do not do it in any way that might make my worship look less than. By all means have your passion, just make sure it doesn't make anyone uncomfortable. It can be devastating for a young believer to face the condemnation of those deemed mature in the faith. George Whitefield says this in regard to the religious crowd's attempt to silence Bartimaeus: "Opposition comes closest when it proceeds from those who are esteemed followers of the Lamb."[1]

When I first entered ministry, I would jump up and down, cry, shout, and show all sorts of emotion in worship. I don't know how many times I was told that one day I would "mature" and be less emotional. As I started doing missions, specifically work in war zones, there were people who told me that I should "enjoy it now" because one day I would have to settle down and "live a more normal life." (Little did they know, here it is 15 years later, and I am still going to the nations with even more zeal than I had then.) When I began preaching, I continued to passionately yell and jump as the Word of God was and is truly like a fire shut up in my bones. Still then, people would advise me that if I wanted to last long in ministry or ever become "successful," I would need to learn how to calm down. I was told that as a woman preacher it would be better if I stood behind the pulpit instead of moving so much, talked more softly, or even if I wore different clothes. Many times I would take off my heels so that I could be as demonstratively vibrant as my heart felt, and my bare feet were often met with criticism. There were plenty of rebukes for this young, hungry believer, most coming from those considered mature in the faith. Just like in Bartimaeus' story, it was those who could have been and should have been used to propel my faith who often became the greatest hindrance to it.

The (hopefully) well-meaning advice of the crowd essentially attempted to rebuke me into silence. As I reflect on the countless times I could identify with Bartimaeus, there was always one prevailing thought that would overwhelm the sound of all the other voices. A thought that we can clearly see in Bartimaeus and in several others who ran to Jesus in search of healing and freedom.

The thought I had is very simple: "You are *not* my Source!"

You are not the One who died for me. You are not the One who saved me. You are not the One who has my healing. You are not the One my hope is in. You are not the One who has the power to transform. You are not the One who provides for me. You are not the One who opens doors for me. You are not the One who promises to lead me and guide me. You are not the One who has shown me unending mercy and compassion. You are not my Source, Jesus is.

As Bartimaeus was in the tension between the crowd that aimed to silence and the reality of Jesus being close by, he must have had the same tenacious realization. *You are not my Source.* He could spend his life on the side of the road begging the crowd to provide for him, or he could refuse to be moved by human approval in order to seek Jesus.

I have watched this generation flood the altars with tears streaming down their faces. I have seen them weep and break in repentance over their sin. I have watched them dance wildly as His joy overtakes them. I have heard them scream out at the top of their lungs as His Presence overtakes a room. I have heard the deep groans in intercession for God to move among their peers. I have even heard the off-key songs sung without concern for perfection. This generation has had the Bartimaeus cry. It has been sincere, loud, and emotional.

**You are not the One who has shown me unending mercy and compassion. You are not my Source, Jesus is.**

Far too many critics have accused this generation of emotion-alism. Let me ask you this question. Would you rather them be emotional in church for Jesus or emotional in a bedroom with another young person attempting to find acceptance and valida-tion in that which does not satisfy? Would you rather them dance wildly in zeal for Jesus or dance wildly in a bar trying to drown away their sorrows in alcohol? Would you rather them weep over their sins at the altar or would you rather them weep at the funeral of another friend who took their own life?

As this generation has begun to cry out just as Bartimaeus did, it has indeed been the religious crowd who has turned to them and told them to quiet down. It is the professional Christians who have decided that their response to Him was too much. If that has been you, if that has been me, I pray that we would all run quickly to the altar and repent. May we not be to this generation what the crowd was to Bartimaeus.

Bartimaeus sets the example for this generation, for all of us. When the critics try to silence you, when they rebuke you, just cry out *even more*. Bartimaeus shouted out "all the more"! This is what attracts me to Bartimaeus. His determined cry in response to the naysayers is why I call Bartimaeus my spiritual boyfriend. In Barti-maeus I see a response that pleases Jesus. I see the same response in this generation.

What does this look like in your life? Who are those who have tried to silence you? Maybe it's time to cry out again. For me, it means I'll preach even louder. I'll worship even wilder. I'll pray even harder. I'll go even further. I will not stop, I will not quit, I will not back down. Neither will this generation; what about you?

It takes focus and determination to continue to cry out while others are trying to silence you. There is a tenacity that rises up. Sometimes the crowd feels overpowering. I pray that we would all have the resolve inside of us to stand up to the crowd.

## PRAYER

On that note, let's pray. If you have felt the suffocating temptation to work for human approval or if you have felt discouraged by the culture's attempt to rob a generation of true acceptance, then pray this with me.

Father, so many times the opinions of others have had an effect on me. Please forgive me; show us mercy. Help me to stay focused on You even when the crowds are loud, even when the attempts to silence have felt so overwhelming. Give us boldness in the Holy Spirit to know when to cry out even more. Give us the courage to be unmoved by the opinions of others.

I ask that You would give this generation that Bartimaeus cry. That the anointing of Bartimaeus would come upon them and give them radical courage. Lord, would You use this generation as an example of how to stand firm in the midst of opposition.

For everyone reading this book now, I ask for an impartation of boldness and tenacity. Where voices have been silenced, I ask that You would loose them. For those young people reading this, I pray 1 Timothy 4:12 over them that they would not let anyone despise them because of their youth, but rather they would set an example for other believers in speech, in conduct, in love, in faith, in purity. For the women and men who are reading this and have felt that call to preach, to mentor, to disciple, to write, and to use their voice, but have been put down and rebuked over and over again. I pray for a fresh impartation of courage.

God, would You help us to forgive those who have tried to silence them. Let us release them into Your hands and move forward in what You have for us. In Jesus' name, amen.

## Note

1. George Whitefield, "Blind Bartimaeus," sermon, https://www.blueletterbible.org/Comm/whitefield_george/Sermons/witf_027.cfm?a=967052#si_1; accessed June 7, 2023.

# REFLECTION QUESTIONS

1. Have you experienced a time when more "mature" believers quenched your fire for Jesus?

2. Do you need to repent for allowing the opinions of others to replace Him as your Source?

3. Have you ever spoken such "quenching" words to a younger person or new believer?

4. When you see extravagant worship, have you ever felt annoyed or embarrassed?

5. Do you need to repent for any of these attitudes?

6. What kind of extravagant, passionate worship do you feel led to pour out today?

*Chapter 5*

# JESUS HEARS US WHEN WE CRY

*Jesus walks at the speed of love.*
—**Unknown**

*Jesus stopped and said, "Call him." So they called to the blind man, "Cheer up! On your feet! He's calling you."*
—**Mark 10:49 NIV**

*Jesus stopped.*

Those two words catch my attention. What causes Jesus to stop? He is the Word. He is Lord. He is Messiah, and yet throughout Scripture we have moments when Jesus appears to allow Himself to be interrupted. Who is this God-Man who appears at times to have extremely flexible plans? What is it from humanity that would cause Him to pause His journey, to stop what He is doing, and turn toward us?

Jesus often stopped for the unlikely. Jesus would stop for ones whom His own disciples did not think He would stop for. We see this in Mark 10:13-16 as Jesus decides to stop for the little children. The disciples try to whisk the children away, seeing them as an inconvenience, but Jesus finds value in stopping for them. In this brief interaction, you can tell that once again even those who walked daily with Jesus did not fully understand His heart. This became normative for Jesus, consistently giving attention to the ones others so easily ignored. In Mark 5:1-20, we find another such intriguing story when Jesus is approached by a demon-possessed man. For an unknown amount of time, this man had been totally rejected by society, living among the tombs, tortured by the legion of demons that inhabited him. This man was the type most people ran from, but not Jesus. Again, Jesus stops to give attention to this man who is crying out for His help.

Clearly Jesus had a pattern of stopping for those most would not, but what is it about Bartimaeus and several others that caught His attention? It is hard to tell on the surface if it is having the right need, the right heart, or maybe even the right environment. Throughout Scripture there were certain cries that seemed to catch Heaven's attention. Look at some of these remarkable verses.

*A very large crowd of people assembled in Jerusalem to celebrate the Festival of Unleavened Bread in the second month. ...The priests and the Levites stood to bless the people, **and God heard them**, for their prayer reached heaven, his holy dwelling place* (**2 Chronicles 30:13,27 NIV**).

*The Lord said, "I have indeed seen the misery of my people in Egypt. **I have heard them crying out** because of their slave drivers, and I am concerned about their suffering. ...The cry of the Israelites **has reached me"*** (**Exodus 3:7,9 NIV**).

*In my distress I called to the Lord; I cried to my God for help. From his temple he heard my voice; **my cry came before him**, into his ears* (**Psalm 18:6 NIV**).

Apparently there is a cry, there is a sound, that reaches the ears of God and compels Him to action. These are the cries of those hungry for Him to move. It is the desperate sound of those who realize that God alone can save them, heal them, deliver them. When people turn to God alone this can be called the cry of faith. It is the cry that says, "God will move on my behalf!"

Faith is not as abstract as we often make it out to be. Faith indeed has substance and it is evidence, as Hebrews 11:1 (NKJV) says, *"Now faith is the substance of things hoped for, the evidence of things not seen."* Faith is tangible.

> There is a cry, there is a sound, that reaches the ears of God and compels Him to action. It is the desperate sound of those who realize that God alone can save them, heal them, deliver them.

Faith always demands a response; it always precedes actions. James points this out when he says:

> So also faith by itself, if it does not have works, is dead. But someone will say, "You have faith and I have works." Show me your faith apart from your works, and I will show you my faith by my works (**James 2:17-18 ESV**).

Faith often seems to ignore the social norms and even at times logical human advice. If you are not the one in faith, it appears to ignorantly deny truth. Faith by all other accounts, usually except for the one who has it, can be quite extreme. Bill Johnson says, "Faith does not deny a problem's existence, it simply denies it influence." In other words, faith is not denying the present obstacles or reality; it is just submitting to a higher truth—the truth of Jesus Christ. We do not have to deny the statistics about this generation to have faith for them. We aren't ignoring the facts; we just have faith that the Word of God supersedes the facts.

Faith can be seen, it can be felt, and it can be heard. It is evident that faith can be seen by how Jesus responds to the healing of the paralytic when he says, *"And when Jesus **saw** their faith, he said to the paralytic, 'Son, your sins are forgiven'"* (Mark 2:5 ESV). Faith can be felt, which is obvious when Jesus says, *"Someone touched me, for I perceive that power has gone*

> **We aren't ignoring the facts; we just have faith that the Word of God supersedes the facts.**

*out from me"* (Luke 8:46 ESV). Faith can also be heard. It is heard when the centurion says to Jesus, *"Just say the word, and my servant will be healed"* (Matthew 8:8 NIV). This level of faith impressed Jesus. The Bible even states that Jesus marveled at his faith (Matthew 8:10). This is the faith that causes Jesus to stop. This is the sound that demands Heaven's attention.

It is this sound that is heard when Bartimaeus makes that bold declaration, "Son of David, have mercy on me!" I believe Jesus heard a sound that He simply could not resist. Jesus heard the sound of faith. Jesus heard the sound of hunger. He heard the sound of determination. The sound of one who says, "I will do whatever it takes to get His attention." Bartimaeus had made that bold declaration, essentially saying, "You are the Messiah, You are my Source, no matter what anyone else is saying, You have what I need." Bartimaeus refused to be quieted down. Bartimaeus refused to be distracted. Bartimaeus refused to be deterred, and Heaven heard his cry.

The response—Jesus stopped.

Several years ago, I was in Brazil getting ready to preach in a church that I had never been to before. As I prayed about the service, I could not get a sense of what God wanted me to speak on. If you're a preacher, you understand that this is not a great feeling. Your main job is to deliver a message, so you can imagine as the time for service drew closer I became more and more nervous. It didn't help that I did not know the pastor or the church well. I arrived at the church and still had not heard anything from the Lord about what He wanted me to say or do. I attempted desperately to remember something, anything, that I could share and nothing was coming to mind. I wracked my brain for the most recent sermon I preached and still nothing. After the greetings with the pastor, we went into worship. I remember thinking that surely Holy Spirit would tell me something during worship. Again, absolutely nothing. Next thing I knew, they were introducing me as the guest speaker and I was taking steps toward the pulpit. It was then, in the final few seconds before I grabbed the mic, that He spoke one very simple thing. He said, "Ask them what they are hungry for." For you reading this, perhaps you feel relieved for me that an answer came, but in the moment my first thought was, "What in the world am I supposed to do for the other fifty-nine minutes and forty-five seconds of this service?" There is no way that one brief question is going to suffice for an entire service. Having zero other options I nervously, with knees shaking, said over the microphone, "God wants to know what you're hungry for."

What happened next I will never forget. Immediately those in the crowd began to cry out. There were undignified screams of those who wanted Jesus more than anything else. I can still hear the sounds that undoubtedly captured the attention of Heaven. The next hours can only be described as holy. God's Presence rushed into the room in such a mighty way that I and my translator both laid face down on the altar. They would not and could not be silenced, though no one present wanted it to end. His Presence was so weighty that day I wasn't sure when if ever I would be able to get off the floor. For an uncertain amount of time, people continued to cry on the name of Jesus, until I began to hear the sound of movement. As I looked up, people were making their way to the altar.

Many were crying as they threw their glasses on the stage because their eyes had been supernaturally healed as His Presence came. There were so many miracles that occurred that night with no one specifically praying for them.

That day, Jesus stopped.

A sound came out of a church in Brazil from people who were hungry for nothing else but Jesus. A cry that caught the attention of Heaven. A cry that ushered in a manifestation of His Presence.

After Jesus heard the cry of Bartimaeus, He stopped and said, "Call him." This generation is one that is choosing to ignore those who would attempt to silence them. They are refusing to be silenced by the religious majority that would say that their cry is too loud, too passionate, perhaps too irreverent. They have chosen not to listen to the voices that would tell them that Jesus is doing something different or that their generation is too lost and too far gone. As stated in the last chapter, you must be focused on the One you are crying out to and determined to ignore the crowd. This generation will not succumb to the pressure of culture; they will cry out even more and Jesus will stop for them. In fact, Jesus is already stopping for them. He is calling them.

> They would not and could not be silenced, though no one present wanted it to end. His Presence was so weighty that day I wasn't sure when if ever I would be able to get off the floor.

Do you know what I find comical? The very people who had rebuked Bartimaeus then said to him, "*Cheer up!* He's calling you." I would say these people are fair weather friends, and like many of you I have had more than my fair share of them. These are the people who criticize you when things aren't working out the way we thought they would. They are ones who not only can't see the promise that God has given you, they are the antagonists of the promise. They want to stop your dreaming. They want to halt your faith. They struggle to believe that Jesus would stop for you, and they certainly do not want Him to use you. These "friends" will kick you when you are down, but when He begins to fulfill His promises, when He stops for you, when He puts favor on your life, all of a sudden they are your biggest supporters and friends. One minute they are rebuking your cry and the next they are wrapping their arm around you and telling you with excitement that Jesus has called you.

We do not get much insight into Bartimaeus' thoughts about these people around him. To be honest, it appears that he gives it barely any thought. I want to encourage you to do the same. Do not allow the crowd's rebuke or the crowd's cheer to affect you. Bill Johnson puts it best when he says, "If you live by the praise of man, then you'll die by their criticism." Be not overly moved when the masses attempt to deny you or when they sing your praises. Instead, take a lesson from Bartimaeus who stayed focused on just One. He did not stop when they tried to silence him and he did not try to make friends when they encouraged him. He simply remained focused on the movement of Jesus. Perhaps it has become cliché, but we truly are meant to live for an audience of One. This is our place of greatest strength.

In my heart of hearts, I believe this will be the heart posture of this generation. In a culture that has tried to sell them endless feedback in the form of social media followers, likes, and comments, I believe they will listen for the voice of Jesus. While the temptation is to find their value in brand agreements, viral videos, and Tik Tok approval, I believe they will prize the acceptance of Jesus above the approval of others. Many of them have tasted of the false acceptance that the crowd has offered them and they realized it did not satisfy. They have known the devastating flippancy of the virtual world. They have experienced firsthand being loved one moment and canceled the next. This society has not met their needs, and they are focusing in on the One who has what they need.

When you hear the voice of Jesus call you, it no longer matters who tried to silence you. Equally, it no longer matters who has tried to promote you. His voice drowns out all of the chatter. His voice permeates through the cultural noise.

> **Perhaps it has become cliché, but we truly are meant to live for an audience of One. This is our place of greatest strength.**

## PRAYER

Father, give us the grace to live for an audience of One. I pray that right now You would heal the wounds of the crowd. For every time that this reader has been kicked when they are down, falsely accused, and rebuked by those who did not fully know their situations, I pray that You would bring healing to their heart. Help us to forgive them, for truly they know not what they do. Protect us from being moved by the criticisms or the praise of others. May we, like Bartimaeus, release a cry for You today that would catch Your attention. May we come out from all of the noise that culture supplies and lock eyes with You. Lord, hear our cry. Hear our cry for our own lives and for this generation. Amen.

# REFLECTION QUESTIONS

1. When have you experienced Jesus stopping for your cry?

2. What was the sound of your cry at that time?

3. Have you experienced the fair weather friendship of other Christians?

4. Have you ever been a fair weather friend to someone who was crying out in pure faith?

5. In what area are you most vulnerable to being distracted by the opinions of others?

6. How can you return your focus to your audience of One?

# Chapter 6

# TIME TO THROW OFF THE COAT OF ENABLEMENT

*Throwing his cloak aside, he jumped to his feet and came to Jesus.*
—**Mark 10:50 NIV**

Immediately after Bartimaeus finds that Jesus has called him, he throws off his cloak. Initially, that does not sound like a point worth mentioning; however, it reveals yet another remarkable layer to Bartimaeus' story and what God is saying about this generation.

Possibly throwing off the cloak was as simple as attempting to cast off any hindrance to get to Jesus quickly. This is both plausible and biblical. In Hebrews 12:1 (ESV) we are even instructed to *"lay aside every weight, and sin which clings so closely"* so that we can continue on in our race effectively. When Bartimaeus throws off his coat, he is indeed casting off what could be a hindrance in his pursuit of Jesus, but what if there is more to it than that?

Dr. Craig Keener explains that the "cloak" that Bartimaeus had was a beggar's coat. It would not only be used as coat for the cold weather, it would also be used for bedding, possibly even used to spread before him as he was begging to catch the donations that would come his way.[1] During this time period, the Roman Empire would give an identification item as proof for a "legal beggar." For someone like Bartimaeus, he would likely have received a beggar's coat as his sign that he was legally disabled, unable to work, and allowed to beg for provision. In other words, Bartimaeus' coat gave him his only means of provision. You could minimally compare it today to having a handicap placard for your car that allows you to park in reserved parking close to the building. Though it is a present day example, it does not give the full extent of the function of the coat for Bartimaeus. Without his beggar's coat, he no longer had a way to legally provide for himself. This coat was the closest thing he would ever have to a paycheck, and the moment Jesus called him he just threw it aside as if it was meaningless.

**This coat was the closest thing he would ever have to a paycheck, and the moment Jesus called him he just threw it aside as if it was meaningless.**

It is easy to skim over this casually, as if to just throw this coat aside was no big deal. This was not one of those altar decisions where you go forward to surrender in the moment and then take it back the next day. It was so much more than that. Bartimaeus again demonstrates a faith that challenges me. When Jesus calls Bartimaeus, he apparently already has an understanding that he will not need that beggar's coat anymore. Ole Barti comes through again in faith. Jesus made no initial indication that He would heal him, but Bartimaeus believed He would.

Once again in the JTV (Jessika Tate Version), I attempt to imagine myself in Bartimaeus' place. He had just undignified himself in front of a mass of people to catch Jesus' attention. He yelled like a maniac only to immediately receive rebuke. Then he heard those words—those two words. Those words carried hope. Those words were transformative. Those two words came with them the resolve that Bartimaeus had believed for. Two simple words.

"Call him."

In an instant, a realization must have occurred that his life would never be the same again. He might not have a full understanding of what this really meant, but obviously he knew that healing was coming. I can imagine him taking that coat and tossing it to the ground as if to say to the crowd, *"This coat is no longer my identity!"*

What the world had previously used to identify him, he easily tossed to the ground once he knew that he had Jesus' attention. Have you ever had an experience like this? I remember right before I began university I had decided to go to a Christian camp for college students the week before classes started. I had encountered Jesus at sixteen, and as I left for university I was not sure what those next few years would hold for me. In the United States most people think of university as the time to "sow your wild oats." It is a time when you can party, drink, and live for yourself before you start real life. In my gut I knew I did not want to do that; I just struggled to know if living for Jesus throughout university was even possible.

One night at this camp, I felt a pull from Holy Spirit to go into their twenty-four-hour prayer room. It was in the middle of the night with just a few students there. As soon as I walked in, I felt His Presence so strongly that I dropped to my knees. Right then and there He spoke to me. I remember weeping at the thought that He sees me. He sees my heart for Him and He sees my fears. In that moment, I threw my coat off. I decided that no matter what people would think of me, whether I had friends or not, Jesus would have all of me. There was something about knowing that He saw me in that moment that transformed everything.

What would happen if we realized what it really meant to have His attention? I am reminded of a song that was popular several years ago from Bethel Music titled "You Don't Miss a Thing."

> What a mystery
> That you notice me
> And in a crowd of ten thousand
> You don't miss a thing
> Cause you see everything
> And I am seen
> And I am known
> By the king of kings
> And lord of lords
> There's no place I can go

Your love won't find me
No place I can hide
That you don't see
No place I can fall
Your love couldn't catch me
You see it all, you see it all
Through the eyes of love

When we realize that Jesus sees us, it should transform the way we view ourselves. Five minutes prior and Bartimaeus was just a disabled beggar. As soon as Jesus called him, he knew he was no longer going to be a beggar anymore. I would even suggest that Bartimaeus stepped into a revelation that he hadn't even fully experienced yet. Bartimaeus went from blind beggar to healed son in an instant. Why? Because Jesus called him.

It is the time when this generation is throwing off their beggars' coats. I see them tossing aside the identity that has been given to them by statisticians, pastors, religious crowds, and cultural leaders. I see them casting off the false lies they have believed about themselves. They have heard Jesus calling them. They have seen that His face is turned toward them and they are responding. They are responding by refusing to be identified by their previous labels. Just as Bartimaeus tossed aside that coat, they are getting free, and they are running to the feet of Jesus. Bartimaeus jumped

**What would happen if we realized what it really meant to have His attention?**

to his feet and he came to Jesus. He came to the One he had cried out for. He ran to his Messiah.

Isn't this real revival? To cast it all aside and run to Jesus. To come face to face with our Savior. Trusting Jesus to revive, restore, and liberate us. This generation is running to His side.

I remember sitting in a gathering that was led primarily by Gen Z. A young woman stepped up to the microphone and boldly said, "I was anxious, I was depressed, I was suicidal, I was everything this world has said about us, then I met Jesus. One thing I know for sure, this generation is breaking free of all of those labels!"

I echo her sentiments, and that leads me to a question for you. What is your beggar's coat? What is the identity or label that has been put on you that says you're not good enough or talented enough? What is the belief you have had stamped on you by your parents, friends, or society? Maybe it is time to throw off the coat.

The reality is we have all had labels placed on us. We have all had moments when people told us that for whatever reason we were unqualified. Those barriers can feel weighty and even ominous. When we can feel the restraint of that "coat," we need a mindset shift. One of my favorite stories is that of Roger Bannister. On May 6, 1954, Roger threw off the coat and broke through a barrier that the world had called impossible by running the very first sub-four-minute mile. Runners had attempted to achieve this milestone since 1886, and by the time Roger came on the scene it was considered the Holy Grail of running aspirations.[2] The speculation was that it would take the perfect weather conditions, on a specific type of track, in front of an overly supportive crowd, by an exceptionally trained athlete, and even then it might not be possible at all. There were countless reasons why no one would ever conquer this perceived unconquerable mountain. However, not only did Roger run a sub-four-minute mile, but within two months another person had done the same. Since Roger did the seemingly impossible, there

> **When we throw off our coat and do what we have been told we could not, we open the way for others to do the same.**

have been over a thousand runners who have done the same. What Roger did in three minutes and fifty-nine seconds has now been brought down to three minutes and forty-three seconds as the world's fastest mile.

When we throw off our coat and do what we have been told we could not, we open the way for others to do the same. Sometimes the fight we are facing feels so extreme because the enemy isn't just trying to stop you, he is trying to stop the ripple effect that will come from your freedom. That label placed on you isn't intended to hold just you back; the enemy wants it to hold your children and grandchildren back. You are fighting for far more than just your current circumstances—you are fighting for legacy.

You are meant to throw off that coat and break through limitations that have held people back for generations. You are a chain-breaker and so is this generation. We are seeing through the schemes of the enemy and pressing through to the fullness of who Jesus has called us to be. We will set captives free.

## PRAYER

So, my friend, what do you want to do with your labels? Let's pray together.

> Jesus, right now, highlight every label that we have used to identify ourselves that You did not give to us. Would You show us the lies we have believed about ourselves? Identify the proverbial coats that we have continued to wear.

Take a moment and ask Him for yourself and take the time to write down what He shows you.

> Lord, speak to my friend now and tell them what You say about them. Help them to fully release that old identity and embrace the truths You have for them. Give them the grace to lay aside every hindrance and run with their eyes completely focused on You. In Jesus' name, amen.

### Notes

1. Keener, *The IVP Bible Background Commentary: New Testament,* 156.

2. William C. Taylor, *Practically Radical* (New York, NY: HarperCollins Publishers, 2011), 116.

# REFLECTION QUESTIONS

1. What is your beggar's coat? What is the identity or label that has been put on you that says you're not good enough or talented enough?

2. Have you heard the voice of Jesus calling you?

3. What new identity has Jesus given you?

4. Do you find it difficult to throw off your beggar's cloak? Why? What perceived benefits does it seem to offer you?

5. Do you need to repent for any areas of not trusting that what Jesus calls you to is better?

6. How will you take that step and throw your cloak down today?

# Chapter 7

# POWERFUL QUESTIONS CHANGE LIVES

*The quality of a leader cannot be judged by the answers he gives, but by the questions he asks.*

—Simon Sinek

*"What do you want me to do for you?" Jesus asked him. The blind man said, "Rabbi, I want to see."*

—Mark 10:51 NIV

The first time I sat with this verse I just laughed out loud. The irony of Jesus asking a blind man what he wants done for him. I don't know if you have ever watched *The Chosen* series, but there are moments when I can imagine Jesus exactly like He is portrayed in that series, saying things that would sound funny at first to us, but that somehow actually carry an invitation. I love Jesus. I love His personality. I love how everything He does has purpose. I love how He is able to do things and say things that most of us would never consider.

One of those things is to ask a blind man what he wants done for him. It seems obvious to me. Any blind man would want to see more than he could possibly want anything else. Jesus' question causes me to stop and contemplate a few things. Is Jesus simply being sassy? I hope I do not get emails about this, but my experience with Jesus is that at times He can be. He can be funny. He can ask questions that equally cause me to laugh while challenging my own perspectives. He has indeed been sassy with me countless times, and it has impacted my heart in a way that only He can. Was He trying to prove a point to the crowd? This is something He did often. In fact, at one point He even prayed in a specific way just so that it would benefit those listening to Him (John 11:42). He was known to say or do things in a specific way because of those around Him.

One thing I have learned is that Jesus never asks a question because He does not know the answer. Jesus asks a question usually because we do not know the answer. One of my favorite examples of this in Scripture is taken from a passage we discussed in Chapter 2. It is the story of Ezekiel in the valley of dry bones. God asks Ezekiel, *"Son of Man, can these bones live?"* (Ezekiel 37:3 ESV). Ezekiel does not attempt to even answer God's question; instead, he gives what I believe to be one of the most wise responses in all of Scripture. He says, *"O Lord God, you know."* My favorite translation of that verse comes from the Contemporary English Version:

*"Lord God, only you can answer that."* Ezekiel understood that if God is asking you a question, it is not because He does not know the answer. He does know the answer, and you are about to learn something.

At times the question that Jesus is asking really has nothing to even do with the answer and has everything to do with us. Jesus will ask a question because He wants to challenge us, to empower us, to move us. I have learned to lean in and pay attention when Jesus is asking a question.

So what was Jesus trying to do with Barti? Bartimaeus had likely been disempowered his entire life. Jesus did not ask Bartimaeus what he wanted because Jesus did not know what he needed. He wanted Bartimaeus to stand up in his new identity and state exactly what he wanted from Jesus. Steven Furtick says, "God cannot meet you were you pretend to be, He can only meet you where you are." There is something powerful that occurs when we are able to boldly and vulnerably ask for exactly what we want or need.

> **If God is asking you a question, it is not because He does not know the answer. He does know the answer, and you are about to learn something.**

I wonder what I might respond if Jesus were standing right in front of me asking what I needed. I think at times I would feel the pressure to give a spiritually acceptable answer. Perhaps I would just be dumbfounded, fully uncertain of what I really needed. In one way, Jesus was completely challenging Bartimaeus by asking this question. He could have easily walked up to him, skipped the question, and healed him.

After studying Jesus' question to Bartimaeus for a while, I decided that I would try out Jesus' method with those I disciple. I wanted to see what type of responses I would get when I asked young believers in various situations what they needed or even what they wanted.

One of the most interesting concepts I discovered was about me! I found that there were many times I did not want to *ask* what they needed; instead, I wanted to *tell* them what they needed. I found it was more comfortable for me to look at specific situations in their lives and tell them what I thought they needed as opposed to actually stopping to listen to their thoughts.

There is much to learn from the way Jesus led those around Him. This relationship with Him was not simply "I say, you do," unlike how we often choose to disciple or even parent. Though Jesus had clear instructions, especially for the disciples, He also had plenty of questions. His questions led the disciples on their own journey of discovery. Questions usually require some degree of reflection and thought. Questions when asked in the right way at the right time have a way of impacting us substantially more than giving answers. Jesus used questions to provoke those around Him into deeper truths and even deeper relationship.

I will never forget one the first meetings I ever had with my spiritual father, Michael Brodeur. We were discussing my upcoming role on his team, and he explained to me that he could either be a boss, a mentor, or a father to me. He explained what each would entail and then he looked at me and said, "Which do you want me to be?" The question challenged some of my own fears, insecurities, and pain. It required me to take an in-depth look at what I really wanted from him. It forced me into a greater measure of growth and partnership than if he simply would have told me what he was going to do.

When I finally learned to keep my opinions to myself and ask the people I discipled to tell me what they needed and wanted, I learned a few lessons that I want to share with you.

First was that, shockingly, there are times when what we think people need and what they really need are not the same thing. This is extremely beneficial information to have for a few reasons. In our arrogance of assuming we know exactly what someone needs, we can be completely wrong about what this person actually needs. I know it is as surprising to you as it is to me, but we can all actually make mistakes, especially when making assumptions of another person's needs and desires. There have been countless times I have chosen to help others in a way that fit my own narrative and missed what their hearts truly needed, simply because I did not ask.

On the other hand, even when we are right about what someone needs, if we do not inquire of them what they need, we can start working on something that this person actually does not want help for or, more specifically, does not want our help for. I'm not saying that there are not times as leaders when we have insight and wisdom that definitely needs to be shared. I am certainly not suggesting

> **There are times when what we think people need and what they really need are not the same thing.**

that there are not times as leaders when we need to use our discernment and intervene. It just seems that if we are going to be Christian leaders, we should indeed take some of our cues from how Jesus led the disciples.

A quick review of the Gospels shows us a Jesus who knew when to give clear instruction and when to ask questions. He knew when to interrupt someone's plans and when to let the natural consequences of life play out. He led in a dynamic way that went far beyond most of the leadership styles we see today.

When I first started asking what those I discipled needed, I realized how often my own pride as a leader became involved. My mentality was that I was older, I had more experience, I was the one discipling the other person, let me do my job and tell you what you need. Perhaps this is how you lead others and even how you have been led in the past. Isn't it frustrating though? When we sit with this verse, we must admit that Jesus Christ, the Son of God, the Wise One, humbly asked Bartimaeus a question. This Philippians 2 Jesus who is our great example of leading, serving, and loving in humility chose not to tell Bartimaeus what he needed; instead, He asked him.

The second thing I discovered by adjusting my method and asking the question was that there were times when people do not know what they need or don't know how to communicate their needs. I realized that many times young people are rarely asked what they need. This question often would leave those I discipled thoroughly puzzled. When we choose to sit in that moment instead of interject our thoughts, we can produce some beautiful outcomes.

It helps us to see what is important to them, not just what it important to us.

It empowers them to make a decision for themselves instead of just relying on others to make decisions for them.

It builds trust in the relationship.

Jesus was not being sarcastic or ignorant when He asked Bartimaeus what he needed; He was empowering him. The man who had been a powerless blind beggar, utterly dependent on the crowd, was standing before the Messiah and Jesus chose to empower him. When Jesus asked Bartimaeus what he needed, He was essentially saying, "You have the power, Bartimaeus, to choose what it is you want in this moment."

We should learn from this moment. We need to be humble enough to ask those we lead what they need as opposed to always telling them what they need. I want to look for opportunities to empower this younger generation instead of repeatedly exerting my authority over them.

I know that if you are reading this book, you want to see this generation empowered, so it should start with us empowering them. I truly believe that this generation is accepting the empowerment of Jesus. Just as Bartimaeus responded with boldness and clarity, this generation is doing the same. Barti did not turn to the people he once needed to ask their opinion; he spoke directly with the One who had his answer.

We have already seen glimpses of this generation stepping into the fullness of what Jesus has called them to. Young leaders are rising up all around the globe. They are hungry, focused, passionate, and ready to usher in this next wave of revival.

Bartimaeus responded, "Rabbi, I want to see."

Many theologians suggest that Bartimaeus' response implied more than just his desire to physically see—he wanted to see spiritually too. Not surprisingly, this generation is crying out with the same request of Bartimaeus.

"Lord, we want to see."

## PRAYER

Lord, I can't think of any better words to end this chapter than to echo the request of Bartimaeus. Lord, we want to see. Help us to discern when to tell and when to ask. May we be led by Your Holy Spirit into greater discovery as we learn to humbly ask questions just as You did. We want to be humble like You. We want to lead others into empowerment as You did. May we learn from You in Jesus' name. Amen.

## REFLECTION QUESTIONS

1. Have you ever had leaders try to tell you what you needed or wanted rather than ask? Were they right or wrong?

2. Have you ever caught yourself telling a younger person what they need, without asking for their thoughts first?

3. Whom do you need to begin asking questions of today?

4. Have you ever been surprised to hear a young person express their needs or wants, finding them to be different from what you thought or expected?

5. Do you ever feel confused about what you need from Jesus or uncertain if your needs are okay to ask of Him?

6. If Jesus asked you, "What do you need?" what would you ask Him for?

# Chapter 8

# FOLLOWING JESUS ON THE WAY

*Outside of Christ, I am only a sinner, but in Christ, I am saved. Outside of Christ, I am empty; in Christ, I am full. Outside of Christ, I am weak; in Christ, I am strong. Outside of Christ, I cannot; in Christ, I am more than able. Outside of Christ, I have been defeated; in Christ, I am already victorious. How meaningful are the words, "in Christ."*

—Watchman Nee

*"Go," said Jesus, "your faith has healed you." Immediately he received his sight and followed Jesus along the road.*

—Mark 10:52 NIV

The culmination of all of our previous chapters finds a climax here as we finally see the result of Bartimaeus' extravagant faith. He is healed. The excessive cry of faith from a beggar bore fruit. We find it difficult at times to deal with Jesus' responses to these situations. Clearly, He says to Bartimaeus, "Your faith has healed you." This is obviously not the only time that Jesus makes this statement in Scripture. We also see it in other passages like the woman with the issue of blood (Mark 5:34), the ten lepers (Luke 17:19), and the centurion's servant (Matthew 8:13).

There is indeed a connection between our faith and the activated power of Heaven. Hebrews tells us that "*without faith it is impossible to please Him*" (Hebrews 11:6 NKJV). I do not pretend to grasp all of the theological intricacies of faith or how it operates, but I will without a doubt say that faith initiates the miraculous. As Jesus said to Bartimaeus, "Your faith has healed you."

Reflecting on Barti's initial cry to catch the attention of Jesus, his refusal to be silenced, his casting off of his coat, undeniably he had faith. He not only had faith in Jesus' ability, he also had faith in Jesus' nature. When we look at Luke 5 and the story of the man with leprosy, we see a different story.

> *While he was in one of the cities, there came a man full of leprosy. And when he saw Jesus, he fell on his face and begged him, "Lord, if you will, you can make me clean"* (**Luke 5:12 ESV**).

Here we find a man who had confidence in Jesus' ability and yet was not so certain of His nature. He says to Jesus, "If You will, You can." I find myself often just like the man with leprosy. I know that I know that God can, but the question that hinders me is, "Will He?" Bartimaeus, though he had no previous personal interaction with Jesus, was willing to risk it all believing that Jesus could and would heal him. Faith will often pull the "not yet" into the "now" and the unseen into the seen. Even when Bartimaeus was blind, he saw through the eyes of faith.

Bartimaeus' faith reminds me of what Romans speaks of Abraham, *"No unbelief made him waver concerning the promise of God, but he grew strong in his faith as he gave glory to God"* (Romans 4:20 ESV). Bartimaeus and Abraham both saw beyond what was rational naturally and instead chose to believe for the impossible. They did not waver in the midst of contradictory circumstances or setbacks. The next verse says of Abraham that he was *"fully convinced that God was able to do what he had promised"* (Romans 4:21 ESV). He clung to faith even in the face of adversity.

Immediately after Bartimaeus asked for his sight, he was healed. Jesus did not lay hands on him or send him on a faith project; He simply said that his faith had already healed him. The term used is actually the word *sozo*, which has a much deeper meaning than just to simply heal. In its fullness it means to save, to deliver, and to make whole. Bartimaeus was made whole.

As he opened his eyes for the very first time, the very first person he saw was Jesus. Could you imagine having a more captivating, overwhelming, life-changing first look? Having been in darkness his entire life, the first ounce of light quite literally comes from the Light. Face to face with the Messiah. It moves me to tears to think of this moment.

Similarly, when I read the creation story I can't help but try and imagine what Adam must have felt in his first few seconds of life. Having been formed from dust, the first breath that he breathes comes straight from the breath of God. As he opens his eyes for the first time, he is looking in the face of his Creator. Again, face to face with God. This is exactly how and what we were created for. A long stare into the eyes of the One who puts breath in our lungs.

When Bartimaeus' eyes see for the first time, he can finally physically see what his spiritual eyes had already shown him. This Man is the Son of God. The passage tells us that although Jesus had told Bartimaeus to "go," Bartimaeus chose to follow Jesus that day. In other passages of Scripture, we see people who are healed and then continue on their own way. For example, when the ten lepers are healed, only one even comes back to say thank you (Luke 17:11-19). Something was different for Bartimaeus. When he looked into the eyes of his Savior, he saw something he could not possibly turn away from. He was captivated. And he was compelled to follow.

> **This is exactly how and what we were created for. A long stare into the eyes of the One who puts breath in our lungs.**

When I sit with this encounter, I think about my own. One of my favorite questions to ask people is, "What is your Jesus story?" If I had the ability this would be the place where we would stop and sit down to chat about how you first met Him. As believers in Jesus, we all have a different story; however, there is one consistent component that always remains the same. Somewhere in your life, He showed up for you. Maybe your story is as dramatic as blind Bartimaeus—you had spent year after year destitute, alone, and afraid—or perhaps like some of my friends you grew up in a Christian home. No matter what your story is, He came for you. I was sixteen years old when He transformed everything. Every single moment of my life since that day has been marked by that one encounter. There is not a single day that has gone by that wasn't impacted by Him. He changed everything for me. He "*sozo*'d" me, if that is even a word.

When I reflect on my truly life-changing encounter with Jesus, Bartimaeus' response is honestly the only one that makes sense. He'd thrown off the coat and refused to go back to "normal." We do not get to hear about what happened with Barti in the following days. In my gut I know he was never the same again. Life as normal was ruined in the most beautiful way.

I meet people all the time who tell me they are frustrated because following Jesus is often unpredictable and mostly uncomfortable. They find themselves fighting to find "normal" in the midst of giving their total yes to Jesus. The ironic thing is that once you become a believer in Jesus, comfort is never promised. The truth is we would not need a Comforter if we stayed inside our comfort zone. He gave us the Comforter because He has every intention of leading our lives into the uncomfortable. We cannot find normal because once Holy Spirit, the actual Spirit of God, dwells on the inside of you, then you are no longer normal. The attempt to be merely human is futile. Please do not misunderstand me—I am confronted with my humanity often. It is not difficult to see my frailties; just come hang out with me for a couple of hours. However, the very same Spirit who raised Christ from the dead now dwells in us. I simply cannot be normal (Romans 8:11). I have found that many people are overwhelmed because they try so hard to fit in and be normal

## We would not need a Comforter if we stayed inside our comfort zone.

while Holy Spirit is inside trying to make them anything but normal.

Bartimaeus appears to be totally uninterested in going back to normal. He again abandons all to follow Jesus. Having only known Him less than a few minutes, he makes the decision to stay by His side. He has no consideration of his former life and looks forward to what is ahead. We would do well to imitate Bartimaeus' faith-filled, total surrender. Without taking the time to measure the cost and instead going onward with Jesus.

This is the surrender of this generation. Once they see His face, they easily abandon all else. They have deeply embodied Jesus' words in Luke 9:62 (ESV): *"No one who puts his hand to the plow and looks back is fit for the kingdom of God."* Many in this generation have encountered Him and they refuse to look back. In fact, many times one of the biggest mistakes we make in the church is to try and make Christianity easier for this next generation.

In the book *Faith for Exiles,* two researchers, David Kinnaman and Mark Matlock, tell us that their findings portray a generation that is ready to sacrifice for their faith.

The church is one of the least demanding environments for young people, in terms of what they are asked to do mentally and emotionally and of what is expected of them when it comes to serving and giving.

We're just so happy to have them there! Yet one of the most hopeful findings in our research is this: young exemplar Christians are more willing to be challenged than the church is willing to challenge them. This means they expect to be asked to do more but in reality experience a faith community that doesn't ask all that much of them.[1]

Jesus required His disciples to leave everything behind to follow Him. We have stepped away from requiring much from this young generation because we're so afraid of losing them. However, maybe they're looking for a faith, a church, that thinks Jesus is worth giving your life for.

After Bartimaeus was healed, he left the old life behind and followed Jesus. This generation is doing the same. They are abandoning all that was "normal" for a life of total abandonment to Christ. May we not water down the Gospel trying to catch a generation that is pursuing Jesus with real faith.

## PRAYER

God, help us to abandon all to follow You just as Bartimaeus did. Let us encourage a generation that You are worth leaving everything behind. If there is anything the person reading this book has held on to, may we follow the example of Bartimaeus and leave it behind. May we join in with the younger generation hungry for a real encounter with Jesus that will change our lives from the inside out. Help us to rid ourselves of the idea of living a normal life. All for You, Jesus. In Jesus' name, amen.

## Note

1.  David Kinnaman and Mark Matlock, *Faith for Exiles* (Grand Rapids, MI: Baker Books, 2019), 51.

# REFLECTION QUESTIONS

1. What is your Jesus story?

2. How did Jesus show up for you?

3. Is there anything you are still holding on to that you need to leave behind to follow Him?

4. Have you been one of the ones struggling to find a "normal" faith in the midst of an unusual calling?

5. Do you trust the Comforter, the Holy Spirit, to sustain you through the things He is asking you to do?

6. How much does your church expect from the young people who attend there?

# PART 2

# THE COMING REVIVAL

*Chapter 9*

# PROTOTYPES
# OF REVIVAL

In February 2023, a few students at Asbury College were so hungry for more of God that they lingered in worship for hours after their chapel service had concluded. Leaders of the university discerned that this was not just an ordinary extended worship time. What started with around twenty students turned into over one hundred students by the end of the day and then over fifteen thousand visitors in one week. For more than two weeks there was round-the-clock worship, prayer, and pursuit of God.

There has arguably been an asinine amount of criticism surrounding the events that took place at Asbury. Every move of God has a certain amount of disapproval, but from my standpoint this particular outpouring had far less of the typical controversial manifestations and issues than past revivals or outpourings and still managed to have the same amount of criticism.

About three days into this outpouring, a few friends and I hopped in a car and took the trip up to Asbury. Let me start with a disclaimer that we were only there for a short period of time, although I have friends who are on staff or spent significantly more time there than I did. My friends and I were uncertain of what to expect because at the time there was not much information being shared about the specifics of what was happening inside the chapel. The building was almost to capacity, but it was before Asbury became a trending topic across social media platforms so it was easily possible to grab a seat in the early evening. Our hearts were hungry to see what God was doing in this precious moment. When we walked in the room, the first thing I noticed was the fact that there were at least forty young people on the stage appearing to be leading the room. There did not seem to be one "main" worship leader or speaker. As the evening continued on with the sweet Presence of Jesus tangible, I was shocked as I noticed what I could only consider a miracle. For hours upon hours, these young people stayed on the platform, engaged in worship, not checking their phones—that is a miracle if I have ever seen one!

As the evening turned into night, the majority of the people left as these hungry college students stayed. The older leaders went back to their homes, but these young people continued to press into worship throughout the night. Their sheer hunger for Jesus reminded me of Joshua, who would stay inside the tent, obsessed with the Presence of God, long after Moses returned to the camp (Exodus 33:11). Just like Bartimaeus, I saw a group of young people with a cry in their heart that said, "If Jesus is moving, then I will not let Him pass me by!" In response, I believe, Jesus stopped. His Presence came in waves day in and day out in the Asbury Chapel.

The night that our group was leaving Asbury, church vans from all over the country were showing up to little Wilmore, Kentucky, to get a taste of what God was doing there. The very night that we left, the leadership decided to open one of the other campus chapels to facilitate the masses that were gathering. There were so many people trying to get into the chapel that speakers were set up outside for those in line to listen in. At one point people were waiting up to eight hours hoping to get a seat inside. The hunger of those few Gen Z college students initiated a move of God that went on to touch the nations. Within one week, Asbury went viral.

For a generation that has been deemed as lost, there was an undeniable fervency to pursue Jesus. Multiple times throughout the outpouring, space was made for testimonies to be shared from the front. There were countless stories of young people who were convicted of their sin and gave their lives to Jesus; others who, once exposed to the Presence of God in that measure, chose to rededicate their lives to Him and fully surrender their lives. I can't remember how many testimonies I heard of anxiety, depression, and even suicidal thoughts leaving. The fruit from the continual worship time was being seen.

This should not be shocking to us. The Presence of God transforms lives. Holy Spirit takes the broken, the sinful, the addicted,

> **This should not be shocking to us. The Presence of God transforms lives.**

**I, for one, do not want to minimize God's ability to transform a life in one instant in His Presence.**

the jaded, and He forgives, heals, sanctifies, and revives. That is revival—hearts being revived to Jesus Christ. Much of the disagreement surrounding Asbury had to do with how much the Gospel was being preached (or the lack of it), if repentance was occurring, and essentially the glaring question, "If all they are doing is worshiping, is that enough to call it an outpouring?" I would first comment that the Gospel was being preached, people were repenting, and much more was happening every day in addition to hours upon hours of Christ-centric worship; however, in spite of that, are we going to argue with a generation of young people that their way of pursuing Christ in humble adoration is inadequate? I, for one, do not want to minimize God's ability to transform a life in one instant in His Presence, just as He did Bartimaeus, just as He did me, just as He has done an innumerable number of times.

After things calmed down from the Asbury Outpouring, I reached out to Greg Haseloff, the university pastor and associate dean of spiritual life at Asbury College to gather more information from behind the scenes of what occurred at Asbury. Greg happened to be the pastor of the Wesley Foundation at Texas Tech University, which I attended while I was in university an unmentioned number of years ago. These are my questions and his responses with regard to Asbury and Gen Z.

**1.** *Can you give us a short reflection on what occurred the first day that the Asbury Outpouring started?*

On Wednesday, February 8, we were focusing on the third or fourth chapel in a series titled: "Love in Action." The series was moving through Romans 12–14, and seeking to unfold an orthopraxis of "loving your neighbor as you love yourself." Our Gospel choir was leading us in worship, and Zach was preaching on Romans 12:9— essentially laying out how we fall short of loving one another if it is not the love of God moving through us.

As chapel closed that morning, no students responded to an altar call. About thirty students remained after the vast majority went to class following chapel. The students lingered and continued to sing for another 20 to 30 minutes—sweetly being with Jesus and responding to the Holy Spirit. During that time about a dozen of them came to the altar and prayed. For those who were in the room, there began to be a sense that the Spirit of God was moving in a special way, that many would describe as the manifest presence of God—often described as "the cloud of God falling on us." One student shared a testimony of hope. The Gospel choir responded to the movement of the Spirit and kept leading the praise. When classes dismissed before noon, a few more students trickled back into the room. After lunch another handful of students filtered in. Between 1 and 2 PM more students migrated back in to Hughes Auditorium, hearing from friends a description that Jesus was present, worship was continuing, and they were encountering the love of God in a special way—sweet, filled with peace, and authentic. By late in the afternoon and early evening, much of campus was aware that "chapel had continued." This didn't mean that all students came back to the auditorium. Some had responsibilities, others knew that for one reason or another they weren't being drawn there. However, the movement of worship, the peace of Jesus' presence, and the clear sense of the love of God being poured out confirmed that worship would continue.

**2.** *What made you and the other leaders decide to let the students continue to stay in the chapel that day?*

Our students experience Hughes Auditorium as a place of worship, not limited to morning chapels on Monday, Wednesday, and Friday. When students are seeking God—whether singing in praise, or prayerfully at the altar—our chapel team, spiritual life team, faculty, and other leaders make room for how God is at work, for our students' genuine seeking after the presence of God. While some students certainly had classes to attend, leaders would typically not interrupt the continuation of worship expressions. In the ethos of our community on campus, we seem to have an implicit trust between students and faculty/staff who discern and respect how God is at work. All those involved in the spiritual leadership of chapel were unified. The calling was to steward the presence of God and follow what the Spirit of God was orchestrating.

3. *What are some of the attributes that you would consider unique to the Asbury outpouring?*

The first and maybe most obvious would be the uniqueness of this move of God among college students. This outpouring of His Spirit has been upon Generation Z, which in American culture has been viewed as a generation of declining faith—the least amount of belief of any generation.

Second, the vibrancy of the worship. The joy that filled the worship and the peace that filled the room during more gentle times were both so authentic and rich that one can only imagine that joy and peace were "displacing depression and anxiety." Joy and peace were being elevated in our worship, juxtaposed to the polarization being elevated in society. Jesus was moving toward our brokenness and fractures in the midst of a world that perpetuates the fractures. The Lord was present, imparting peace to a generation, and a world, that has struggled to know peace.

Third, a unique attribute was the "lack of production," which was expressed as simplicity in the leading of worship. This included no words on the screens and no high-tech production of what was unfolding on stage. This attribute means very little in the history of awakenings and revivals, yet it is worth reflection

> **Jesus was moving toward our brokenness and fractures in the midst of a world that perpetuates the fractures.**

in this cultural moment of the last fifty years. As production can garner too much attention in the church—and as cell phones skyrocket our distraction thousands of times per day, 24/7—suddenly an old auditorium with stained-glass windows filled with desperate, hungry college students thirsting for righteousness captured our attention. Jesus actually captured our attention, and it seems this particular attribute eliminated peripherals that have often distracted us—in order that Jesus could more completely and fully receive our attention!

Fourth, worshipers coming for consecration. Encounters at the altar were marked by people's desire for their lives to be fully consecrated. Being delivered from pornography addiction, alcohol, drugs, or other addictions came because people where thirsting for complete purity. The words over the altar are *Holiness unto the Lord*—and this was the hunger within the people at the outpouring. They came to have their lives consecrated and completely surrendered to the Spirit of God filling them with holy love.

A fifth attribute of this outpouring might relate to diversity—generational diversity, ethnic diversity, and international diversity. Attendees were of all ages. In the first week the worshipers created prayer huddles for the younger generation to pray over the older generation and for the older generation to pray blessing over the younger generation. The people gathered for worship were of many races, and the outpouring included many international attendees from every continent in the world. Flags from multiple continents were visible over and over again—in particular at two of the venues.

Last, the timing of the outpouring in the midst of a country experiencing deep polarization and a world that is roughly one year beyond the Covid-19 pandemic is interesting. The emotional healing, reconciliation, hope, and joy many received certainly qualifies as a unique attribute during the cultural climate of 2023.

### 4. *In your opinion what made the Asbury outpouring go viral?*

While none of us can answer this question with certainty, a couple of key factors might be at work. Followers of Jesus do trust He is Lord over all—for "from Him are all things, and to Him are all things"—so He can receive the glory from a viral movement. The world is looking for hope and desperate for an authentic move of God, which seems to play a role in how many had their attention captured by this work of God. Lastly, the simplicity that was visible appeared to validate the genuineness of God's presence. For example, the worship was joy-filled and low-tech. The singing was so rich, boisterous, filled with celebration, and exalting of Jesus' name. Often people would say, "I couldn't leave because of the presence of Jesus and the singing." The music had very little production and no lyrics were being projected. The bands were not leading times of worship that were highly produced. The absence of streaming worship and the simplicity of what was captured apparently played an intriguing role in the viral movement.

**5.** *In your personal opinion, would you rather this time be called a revival, outpouring, or does it even matter?*

There is a recognition of what unfolds in John 9 when the disciples asked, "Who sinned, this man or his parents, that he was born blind?" Jesus responded that "This happened so that the works of God might be displayed in him." Whatever the events of February might be called, we know that the works of God were displayed.

I have a preference of this particular move of God being called an outpouring. As we listened to how people were encountering this move of the Holy Spirit and how people experienced attributes of this awakening, we sensed it was an outpouring of God's love, peace, and presence. The word *revival* is a word that is on equal footing with *renewal* and *awakening*—though the most accurate use of any of these words may await more time to discern the fruits of the movement. Revivals can be planned or spontaneous, and can take on a wide variety of expressions depending on the particular stream of Christian tradition. In order to move beyond some of these realities, we've most often described this special time an outpouring.

**6.** *Why do you think God picked Asbury, or would you explain it in a different way?*

The timing and place of God choosing to encamp and tabernacle comes with significant mystery. We do know that college students have been crying out for God to bring revival, renewal, and awakening on the college campus and to their generation. College students hungering and thirsting for righteousness, who were lingering and waiting for God, were the forerunners of this movement. We might ask the question with less emphasis on "where" and more emphasis on "who." Who was it that was desperate for God to move and most desiring of His presence?

> **College students hungering and thirsting for righteousness, who were lingering and waiting for God, were the forerunners of this movement.**

### 7. *Would you say that this move was predominantly student-led?*

Yes. Students were clearly at the forefront. They were the intercessors, the lead worshipers, the men and women hungry for purity, seeking to be filled with holy love, and the ones saying yes to being sent as carriers of the good news of Jesus. Would they say they were the only ones? I don't think so. Every generation of Jesus' followers is acutely aware of two realities—they are connected to believers who have gone before them and invested in them, and they are called to disciple and love those who are coming after them. The movement began with the Spirit of God being poured out on college students hungering and thirsting for righteousness; among college students who had interceded for the Spirit of God to bring awakening, renewal, and revival on university campuses; and among college students acutely aware of their own brokenness and need to receive salvation, purity of heart, healing from anxiety and depression, deliverance from addictions, secure identity in Christ, and a confident calling to be ambassadors of good news. In these realities of being predominately student-led, the students at the front of the movement were grateful and connected to the transgenerational beauty of the body of Christ.

## 8. *Why/how was the decision made to let the students continue to lead?*

Regarding worship teams, students leading is very natural and congruous with our university rhythms. They are often our worship leaders. When it came to other elements of worship like Scripture and prayer, their leadership was central and in the flow of what God was doing in this movement. We sensed less of a decision, per se, but rather we were on a quest of stewarding the presence of God that included discerning what God was doing. We had complete unity in naming that the movement began with college students, was in very significant ways for college students, and that the leadership of college students would be instrumental in the spread of this movement unfolding with Gen Z on campuses across the country and the world.

**9.** *What were some of the pros/cons to allowing students to lead in something like this?*

All of the pros are expressions of new wineskins. The church's prayer for a movement of God among young people is absolutely dependent upon young people leading the movement. Students will affirm how powerful the sharing of testimonies was during the outpouring. Every time testimonies were shared, we quoted Revelation 12:11: "They triumphed over him by the blood of the Lamb and by the word of their testimony." So we could also understand this verse as a declaration that we can triumph over the enemy's attack on the students' generation by the word of their testimonies. Students experienced the work of Jesus in their life overcoming their fears; overcoming identity crises; overcoming anxiety, depression, pornography. Their leadership and their voice was more than a positive—their voice was essential. Students are more than the church of tomorrow—they are the church of today!

> **Students are more than the church of tomorrow—they are the church of today!**

10. *Would you give any advice to other leaders who want to empower the younger generation?*

First, get out of the way. Second, after embracing the first priority of getting out of the way, discover your purpose as a leader *with* and *beside* college students. College students who are courageously seeking to follow Jesus are also longing to follow Jesus with humility. Humility keeps them interdependent upon the transgenerational gifts in the body of Christ. Older followers of Jesus grow hopeless and grumpy when they lose touch with the presence of God in younger generations. College students grow misdirected and entitled without healthy relationships with older generations of believers. The outpouring included sweet and powerful times of Generation Z praying for their elders and the older generations praying blessing upon blessing over Generation Z.

## OUR RESPONSE

This leaves me with an excitement that just maybe we will see the fulfillment of the prophecies over this generation. That this Bartimaeus generation will rise up and be leaders in this next move of God on the earth. If He is truly calling them the Bartimaeus generation, what if Asbury is a prototype of what God wants to do in the earth? Perhaps the biggest questions are not "what if," but if so, then how should we respond?

# REFLECTION QUESTIONS

1. What kind of reactions from others did you hear concerning the Asbury outpouring?

2. Did you feel skeptical about what you heard because it was an outpouring among college students?

3. Have you ever experienced a "church pressure" to make sure that the Gospel is preached, even if it interrupts a movement of worship?

4. Have you ever seen worship being treated in the church as "less important" than preaching?

5. How would your church respond to a movement among the young people like Asbury?

6. How can you step into a position *beside* young leaders hosting the Presence of God?

# Chapter 10

# WHERE DO WE GO FROM HERE?

*There is an entire section in the bookshop called "Self-Help," but there is no section called "Help-Others."*
—Simon Sinek[1]

*To Timothy, my true child in the faith: Grace, mercy, and peace from God the Father and Christ Jesus our Lord.*
—1 Timothy 1:2 ESV

If God is truly raising up this next generation to play a major role in this next move of God, then one thing is for sure—we have to be ready to make discipleship a priority again. As I look around, I am less concerned with Gen Z embracing the Gospel of Jesus Christ, and I am more painfully aware of our lack of desire to intentionally disciple them. If God has chosen them, where do we go from here?

Several years ago, I had been traveling and ministering with my spiritual mother. After a night when we had ministered together and seen God show up and do some absolutely astounding miracles, I was lying in bed and talking to the Lord. I was telling Him how much I enjoyed ministering alongside her and how I did not want to do ministry alone. For years I had heard the analogy that ministry was like a relay race. The generation before us runs their race and then there is a time when they pass the baton on to my generation. The cycle continues as I will run my race then pass the baton on to the generation after me. It is a good analogy for explaining why we need to ready ourselves and the runners after us to run their race, but it never sat right with me. I didn't like the idea that my spiritual mothers and fathers would get off the track and I would run the race alone. Oftentimes I felt there was a pressure on those older than me to start sooner rather than later planning their exit from ministry. It many times came with the insinuation that there was this ethereal moment when the older generation no longer had anything to offer us in the next generation and apparently we magically had all we needed to carry on this mission. Although there is plenty to be said about the reality that we do have to learn to grow up and run our race, I never could understand why we use an example that implies that we run on the track alone.

That night as I was explaining to God how my favorite moments in ministry were ministering with my spiritual parents or my spiritual children, I fell asleep. I woke up the next morning with a clear word in my Spirit as God said to me, "It was never meant to be a relay race; it is meant to be like roller derby!" The impression was so strong that I knew God was telling me something profound. The problem was I had never watched roller derby in my life. I did what any good millennial would do and I started googling the game of roller derby. When my spiritual mother came into the room, I shared with her what God had shown me and she immediately said it made perfect sense.

Roller derby is a contact sport that is intense and even brutal at times. Players are on the track together with each having different roles. They work together, including the newer and older players as well as those who are quick and others who are strong. Every player has a unique purpose as they fight together for the ultimate goal. Working together is how you win in roller derby. You skate together side by side.

This is an analogy that makes sense to me. Speaking from my own experience, we have so much more strength when we run together. We need the wisdom of the older generation, the youthful energy of the young, and the confidence that comes from knowing someone is running alongside us. There is no biblical foundation for lone ranger Christianity. We must find ways to bridge the perceived gaps we have between the generations.

If you haven't realized it by now, this book is a cry for the generations to come together. It is a plea for the older generation to prioritize discipleship. Now more than ever we need spiritual

> **There is no biblical foundation for lone ranger Christianity. We have so much more strength when we run together.**

mothers and fathers who are willing to invest in this next generation. We need to be prepared to play roller derby. It is time for all
hands on deck, with no more spectators in our churches. I dream
of churches where every person is either discipling, being discipled,
or ideally both.

For too long we have attributed the Great Commission only to
those who are called to go to foreign mission fields. While doing
so we have overlooked the commandment in our own lives: "*Go
therefore and make disciples*" (Matthew 28:19 ESV). So if the Great
Commission includes discipleship, it causes me to ask the question,
"Why isn't more of the church actually doing it?" Almost every single place I go to minister I am asked this exact question or a similar
variation to it. It is such a glaring disparity in what the Bible says
and what the church practices that Dallas Willard wrote an entire
book titled *The Great Omission* addressing the reality that we have
completely skipped this very large and straightforward command
in Scripture. My response to the question is always the same—we
don't do it because it is hard.

True biblical discipleship is messy. It's vulnerable. It's raw. It takes
two people who are willing to truly love each other. It requires being
honest about the real you and the real them. So much confrontation and mercy is required. Pain will undoubtedly occur; there will
be setbacks and disappointments but also growth, intimacy, and
success. Discipleship isn't easy and perhaps that's why we've settled
for the counterfeits and masks. There is no cookie-cutter formula
for how to effectively disciple. Trust me, if there was, I would invest
all I have in advocating it to the body of Christ. We have created

classes, programs, curricula, and more with this desire to try and simplify discipleship, but the reality is it just isn't that simple.

Please, don't hear what I'm not saying. I am not saying throw out every single discipleship course. I think many of these programs and schools are beneficial. In fact, I have created them myself. Often they appear to be a step up from the glaring deficiency we usually have; however, if we are honest with ourselves, when we do biblical discipleship it takes a whole heck of a lot more intentionality than putting someone on the roster of a course. It requires a measure of life-on-life learning.

Discipleship is not effectively done through social media, a Zoom screen, or shockingly even a pulpit. It is not that those avenues do not have their benefits, but ultimately they will not accomplish the goal of making disciples. Why? Because discipleship is not a behavior modification program. Following the law does not equate to biblical disciples. Our goal is not to take everything we perceive as negative from Gen Z and turn them into really great rule followers, consequently following the rules that make us feel superior and safe.

> We give up on discipleship when we realize that there is so much more to it than just assimilation to our way of doing life.

This has been one great challenge in the last decades of the church. We give up on discipleship when we realize that there is so much more to it than just assimilation to our way of doing life. Unfortunately, that doesn't work in a generation that has absolutely no experience in our understanding of how the world works. Their world is different. They have never lived in a society without cell phones and the internet at their fingertips. They have no clue what it means to go to the store to rent a movie, and they have always been able to order fully cooked meals from local restaurants delivered to their doorstep in less than an hour. Steven Robertson makes a strong point in his book about Gen Z called *Aliens Among Us* when he says:

> Other generations demonstrate an initial compassion, but that quickly wears off when the older generations begin to realize just how different this new generation is, when they begin to see that this new generation has no intention of assimilating to their ways of doing things and fitting in to the world they have created.[2]

Gen Z does not want to go backward in their technological boom, and if we are insistent on making them like us we will miss out on the opportunity to truly disciple them. Discipleship is making them followers of Christ with their own unique attributes and assignments, not just forcing them into submission as our own followers who perfectly mimic us. Christ is ever present in their generation, and He is looking for disciples. Will we fulfill the command to disciple them?

We need a return to biblical discipleship. We need an older generation that is willing to mother and father these upcoming revivalists. We need to intentionally disciple them to look like Christ—not just like us. Whether you want to call it spiritual parenting or discipleship, it really doesn't matter to me—I just want us to start intentionally investing in this next generation.

The best way to know how to disciple is to look at how Jesus discipled. In the Gospels I often find a stark difference between how Jesus discipled people and how we do it in the church today. Jesus did more discipleship from the dinner table than from the pulpit. He picked those I would have never picked. He said things that I often think are inappropriate, and there were plenty of times I wish He would have scolded the disciples and instead He told a story. He just did things differently than what I think makes sense, but as we all know you can judge by the fruit, and with eleven of Jesus' disciples He turned the world upside down. Imagine if we learned to disciple as effectively as He did.

I want to give you a few simple keys that have helped me with mothering the next generation and staying focused on discipleship.

## 1. *Discipleship Requires Holy Spirit Guidance and Discernment*

I list this first because of the priority this needs to be as we begin to make disciples. You cannot do this on your own; you need the help of the Holy Spirit. This starts from day one as you try to choose whom to disciple. In my early days of learning about discipleship or spiritual parenting, I was encouraged to pursue those whom I would want to disciple me. In other words, the mentee pursued the mentor. I am not avidly against this concept, but it is not the primary way we see Jesus gain disciples. Sure, there were those who came to Jesus and asked to follow Him (including Bartimaeus), but His main twelve disciples, He chose for Himself! This is actually quite powerful when we come to someone and say, "I choose you!" We are essentially saying, "I believe in you and I want to invest in your life."

What sort of implication does that have for me? I believe that it should inspire us, with the help of Holy Spirit, to pick people to disciple. In Luke 6:12-13 we see that Jesus went out alone and prayed all night long. When He came back from praying, that is when He specifically chose the twelve to be apostles among the other disciples. Jesus knew that this was a big decision that needed to be bathed in prayer. We should take discipleship with the same seriousness. It is not a decision that should be made in the moment and taken lightly; rather, it should be made with prayer and Holy Spirit guidance.

You cannot disciple every young person who is in your environment; therefore, we should be aware of who Holy Spirit is calling us to. I have found myself often guilty of picking people to disciple who appeared to be the best choice on the outside, but in the end the relationship was a massive headache both for me and for them. That is not to say just because problems arise in

**You cannot do this on your own; you need the help of the Holy Spirit.**

discipleship that it wasn't God; however, when things get difficult you want to know that it was God who led you to that person and not your own thinking. I have been shocked over the years at the times that Holy Spirit would highlight someone I would have never thought of and then they became one of those who grew closest to me. On the opposite side, I have spent plenty of time pouring into those He never asked me to. After many failures and successes, I have found that it is best to simply let Holy Spirit choose who you enter into a discipleship relationship with.

I want to encourage you that once Holy Spirit has led you to a specific person to disciple, go and approach them. Be upfront about what you are feeling from Holy Spirit and give them an opportunity to make a decision if they want this type of relationship with you or not. I will often sit down with a person I feel led to disciple and I will lay out for them exactly what I heard Holy Spirit say, what I believe He wants from me and from them, and what they can expect if we choose to do this together. I have adapted Brené Brown's statement for my leadership as she says simply, "Clear is kind."[3] I believe it is kind to be upfront and honest about what people can expect from us. I have seen many spiritual parenting relationships fail because of unmet or misunderstood expectations. This problem may not be completely solved with this opening conversation; it will most likely have to be visited many times as the relationship evolves, but I can guarantee it will alleviate some of the initial tension by being very clear in the beginning. If you can only meet once a week for an hour in your office, let them know. If you are hoping that they will jump in and be part of your family throughout the week, let them know. No matter what you are expecting, make those expectations clear and give them an opportunity to voice theirs as well. Then having the complete picture of what each other is expecting, you can move forward in what Holy Spirit has asked you to do.

Even after we begin the journey of discipleship, our learning with Holy Spirit has only just begun. If you are a parent in the natural, you know exactly what I mean. It is absolutely impossible to be a Christ-like parent, spiritual parent, mentor, or discipler without the help of Holy Spirit. He simply knows what we do not know. He sees what we do not see. He hears what we do not hear, and ultimately He is the best parent. Trying to disciple someone without Holy Spirit is like going on a road trip without a map or GPS. It is futile, and your journey will only end in frustration. As you begin to meet with people to disciple them, do not neglect time in prayer asking for wisdom and discernment from Holy Spirit. You will be utterly amazed at what He will show you. Consistently over the years of discipling young people, I have had Holy Spirit tell me things in prayer that have prevented buckets of tears both from me and those whom I disciple. I am beyond grateful for the help of Holy Spirit in discipleship.

Holy Spirit will always bring people back to Jesus. He will consistently season our speech with the reality of the Gospel of Jesus Christ. When we disciple with Holy Spirit, we make disciples of Jesus instead of ourselves. This is the ultimate goal. We are to disciple people into deep relationship and maturity in Jesus Christ.

## 2. *Discipleship Requires Intentionality*

We already discussed how there is not a cookie-cutter, one-size-fits all program to create disciples. As we study how Jesus discipled people, each of His followers had a relationship with Him that was unique to them. For instance, we don't have a single example of Jesus rebuking John to the degree that He did Peter. When we look at Peter, we see plenty of examples of Jesus calling him out both privately and in front of his peers. Our most recited example of John is him reclining on the bosom of Jesus. It doesn't make his treatment of one better than the other; He just had a different relationship with each of them. What Peter needed was different from what John needed. The things Peter would go on to do were very different from what Jesus asked John to do. In both of their lives, we see that Jesus invested in them and trusted them. Peter went on to be one of the leading apostles in the church, and Jesus trusted John with taking care of His own mother. Who they were as individual people must have been so different, and discipling them required a unique approach for both. This is why I struggle with a class that uses a standardized curriculum and calls it discipleship. It does a great job of delivering valuable information to those who are hungry to learn more, but it does a poor job of bringing transformation in the very specific, tailored-to-you areas that need attention. When we disciple individuals, we must gear our discipleship to the person.

Discipleship should be more people focused than it is ministry focused. What I mean by that is that in many places we have done a tremendous job of making disciples of our ministries. We have people who can quote the core values of our ministry and yet they do not know the Ten Commandments. They are experts at quoting the lead pastors of the movement but couldn't tell you one of the beatitudes. They have all the ministry merchandise, share the clips on social media, and they haven't had alone time with Jesus in months. It is nerve-wracking that we have made disciples of our ministries who are not disciples of Jesus. To make them disciples of Jesus requires that we do more than stick them in a class that helps them assimilate into our ministry. Instead, we take the responsibility of intentionally investing in their individual lives.

### 3. Discipleship Requires Belief

Believing in people brings transformation. Jesus took the unlikely and He did what many of us find it so difficult to do—He believed in them. He took fishermen, a tax collector, sinners, and long before they ever laid hands on a single sick person, He called them, He believed in them. He treated them according to their destiny, not their present condition. Paul does the same thing with Timothy when he treats him according to the prophecies over his life (1 Timothy 1:18). It makes a significant impact on the life of another when we treat them according to who God has called them to be and not just whatever present deficiencies they may have. Many times our greatest mistake in discipleship is assuming that our main role is to find fault in the way that someone is living. We begin to take out our "sin detectors," searching through the details of another person's life just looking for what wrong we can hold them accountable for. Our focus becomes their mistakes, and ultimately we begin to lose belief in their real transformation into Christlikeness.

One of my favorite books I have ever read is a book called *Tattoos on the Heart* by Gregory Boyle. This book is a collection of stories of what can happen when one man decides to believe in others before they have even earned it. Boyle is a Jesuit priest who decided to give his life working in an area of Los Angeles that is heavily impacted by gang presence. Each story in this book will have you in tears as Boyle exemplifies what it looks like to believe in a person. What is convicting is Boyle does this with the people whom most in the church would find it impossible to believe in. Not just a neglected generation but the violent, drug-addicted, oftentimes felons who have engaged with gang culture. Boyle pleads with the church to have a change in perspective. He challenges us to believe in people before we start judging them.

Steven Robertson echoes the sentiment in *Aliens Among Us* when he says:

> A change in perspective always precedes a change in behavior or attitude. When you change the way you think about Gen Z, it will change the way you interact with them, the way you speak into their lives, the way you parent them...and the way you lead them in the workspace.[4]

As we first decide to believe in the individuals we disciple, we will inevitably treat them according to that belief. This generation has had plenty of people who doubt them. Humanity as a whole has had an epidemic of hopelessness. Discipleship requires belief. If we want to see people walk in both the character and power of Christ, we must believe in them.

## 4. *Discipleship Requires Vulnerability*

Most of us despise the reality that if we want true intimacy in relationships, then we must have vulnerability. I will be the first to admit that if there was any way possible for me to have deep, meaningful relationships without vulnerability then sign me up. Put me on the train. I'm all in. Unfortunately, this is impossible. There is risk in relationship. For discipleship to be effectual, we have to get comfortable with vulnerability.

I remember sitting with a leader a few years ago as they explained to me that they wanted to be a spiritual parent, they just did not want to go through the pain they had previously endured due to a spiritual child. I couldn't help but laugh, because isn't that how we all feel? No one enjoys pain unless there is something disturbingly wrong with your mental health. Quite the opposite—most of us will spend our lives doing whatever necessary to avoid pain,

> There is risk in relationship. For discipleship to be effectual, we have to get comfortable with vulnerability.

and here lies the problem. You cannot effectively disciple without experiencing pain. We have all heard it said, "Even Jesus had a Judas." I would take it even further and say Jesus had a Peter who denied Him in the moment that He needed him most. And not only Peter, every single one of His disciples at one point left Him, denied Him, failed Him. Why on earth would I think my story would be any different? To truly love, to truly invest, to get close enough to make any significant impact, we have to open up our hearts and let someone in. We have to make ourselves vulnerable.

Sure you can close off your heart, keep people at an arm's distance away, never let their decisions or words impact you. You can be emotionally unattached and feed them beneficial biblical information, but you will not disciple the way Jesus did. I would suggest you will not make true disciples of Jesus.

Vulnerability takes many different forms, but the way I find it most easy to describe is by simply saying, *Jesus does not meet us where we pretend to be; He meets us where we really are.* If we are to lead people into an encounter with Jesus, grow them into mature believers, then we cannot do that without being honest about where we really are and who we really are. I cannot help you with an issue that you are unwilling to admit you have. As we choose to disciple, we need to stress this to the next generation—this is a place where you must be willing to be vulnerable. You must be honest and upfront. I thank God that Holy Spirit will often show us what is going on in a young person when they have not verbalized it themselves, but I much prefer when they come on their own admission. This is where it gets frustrating. This generation especially will not openly come to you unless they have first seen vulnerability practiced by you. It does not mean we share everything with everyone. To put it frankly, that's stupid. It does mean that we learn to practice vulnerability with safe people in our lives. We demonstrate what it looks like to confess our sins, own our weaknesses, share about our places of pain. We don't model independence; we encourage and embrace community. I cannot expect the ones I disciple to open their hearts and lives with me if I have never given them any example of making myself vulnerable.

As we begin to practice mutual vulnerability, then we have the privilege of embracing people with all of their flaws and weaknesses. I get the privilege of looking at someone's pain and saying, "I see that, I see you, now let's go on this journey of healing with Holy Spirit." I have the distinct honor of seeing someone's sin and shortcomings, then instead of rejecting them I get to forgive them as Christ does, love them as Christ does, show them mercy as Christ does. If I never get to see their weaknesses then I only have the opportunity to love them for their strengths. I want to love people not just for how they benefit me or the ministry, not just for what they positively bring to the table, but for who they are, even in their mess, because that's what Jesus did when He discipled.

**Jesus does not meet us where we pretend to be; He meets us where we really are.**

I am concerned when I see discipleship relationships that look more like an employer and employee than a father or mother with their child. In a working relationship, I fire you as soon as you cease to produce the outcome that I hired you for. In a parental relationship, I work with you to solve the issues in your life because we are family and families fight together.

## 5. *Discipleship Is unto Maturity*

Discipleship is not a relationship just for the sake of making someone feel loved and accepted. Though that is valuable, it is not the sole purpose. We are not discipling you just so you have a safe place to reside within the body of Christ. In fact, I would counter and often say that being a Christian isn't necessarily our version of "safe." My spiritual father puts it this way. If the only mission your family has is to create a safe place for your children to belong, then you will likely end up with your child being forty years old, living in your basement, playing video games, and letting you do their laundry. Why? You created a safe place, but you never facilitated growth or maturity. This doesn't work in the Kingdom of God, and it certainly was not how Jesus discipled. Jesus promises us a Comforter because He has every intention of kicking us out of our comfort zone. We are meant to be maturing, both in our Christlike character and in His power and authority. One of my favorite lines from *The Chronicles of Narnia* is a question regarding Aslan who is the character that is an archetype of Christ. The child asks the beaver, "Is He safe?" The beaver is a little shocked and responds, "No, but He is good."

Becoming a disciple of Christ is so much more than receiving His unconditional love; it is maturing to be like Him. In other words, you should be challenging those you disciple to consistently become more like Christ. At the risk of being repetitive, I want to re-emphasize the quote from *Faith for Exiles*, which I quoted earlier.

> The church is one of the least demanding environ-
> ments for young people, in terms of what they are
> asked to do mentally and emotionally and of what is
> expected of them when it comes to serving and giving.
> We're just so happy to have them there! Yet one of the
> most hopeful findings in our research is this: young
> exemplar Christians are more willing to be challenged
> than the church is willing to challenge them. This
> means they expect to be asked to do more but in real-
> ity experience a faith community that doesn't ask all
> that much of them.[5]

Expecting more requires something that so many of us avoid. Confrontation. I know many leaders who will pray for months to see someone on their staff change their behavior, but they won't ever sit down and confront them face to face. This is cowardly and ultimately does a disservice to those we disciple. We have all seen abuse of power and we know there is an unhealthy, ungodly way to confront people. Alternatively, confrontation can be done in a godly way that leads to true growth and maturity, both for the individual being confronted and the relationship of the two. Jesus did confrontation often. I do not know a anyone who would say that Jesus was non-confrontational. Jesus knew when and how to confront in a way that would best mature His disciples.

This is where we need to grow as those who disciple. Not every person needs to be confronted in the same way. We have to learn how to communicate with the individual in a way that they will best receive it. For years my mindset was, "I am the leader, thus everyone should adapt to my ways." However, when I looked at Jesus I saw that He appeared to adjust His leadership style for the one He was addressing. To some He was blunt, to others He spoke in parables, for some He was stern, and still others He was soft. In every moment, Jesus was led by Holy Spirit to confront individuals according to what would make the greatest impact on them for their specific situation. He did not shy away from their sin or weaknesses, He did not ignore their heart conditions, He matured them with Holy Spirit guidance.

I currently have two girls I disciple who could not be more different in personality. For one, if I merely mention she handled a situation incorrectly she will most likely burst into tears. For the other, if I mention she handled a situation incorrectly, on a good day she is going to ask me a million questions about why it was wrong. On a not good day, she's going to argue to her death for why she handled it the way she did. I cannot confront the two the same. They are both strong leaders with incredible gifting, they both need confrontation, but it must be done in a way that best brings godly reproof to them as individuals.

If we are to disciple people into mature followers of Jesus, then we have to hold them accountable to the standard of the Bible. We cannot water down His words to make them feel more comfortable. This starts by prioritizing His words in our own lives and willingly admitting when we fall short, because we will. If we show them what it looks like to be quick to repent before God and people, then they will do the same. There is no shame in the reality that we still need Jesus. I made it my determination to be uncomfortably repentant before God and others. Not just in front of my peers, but even in front of those I lead. When I do this, then this becomes a relationship that isn't just about them maturing but also about me maturing. I start to give them space to confront me also. Obviously, this was a little bit different with Jesus because He was, well, perfect, and yet still I see that He had the type of relationship with His disciples that Peter felt comfortable confronting Him, even if Peter was way off base. Discipleship shouldn't be one way. It should not just be me correcting them and them doing what I say. It should not just be them serving my vision, when Jesus said that to be like Him we must become a servant. This relationship is meant to mature both of us into greater depths of Christlikeness.

In addition to helping disciples live out the Word of God in character, we should also be showing them how to live out the Word in His power. I find that often depending on the denomination we usually have a bent. There are certain denominations that teach heavily how to obey the Word of God and there are others who excel in teaching people how to operate in the supernatural. To be a disciple of Jesus is to do both. This should be challenging to us. As we make disciples of Jesus, we should first be examples to them of both the character and the power of Jesus. I do not want to attempt to teach someone to exemplify characteristics of Jesus that I refuse to practice myself. Whether we are discussing His integrity or His authority to cast out demons. Together we should be maturing in both.

In order to do this, I have to become comfortable with failure. We do not grow if we do not risk, and I have never met someone who succeeds one hundred percent of the time. As a mother, I often struggle with wanting to prevent every mistake, every failure, and every place of pain in my spiritual children.

> **We have to become comfortable with failure. We do not grow if we do not risk.**

I feel the ache in my heart when I can see an oncoming difficulty, but it's not my job to prevent those I disciple from every mishap. We grow from seasons of tension, we learn from our mistakes, and in pain we often meet Jesus in ways we hadn't before. As someone who disciples others, I believe it is important for us to learn the difference when the people we lead are proverbially about to get a bump on the head from running into a wall or they're about to end up hospitalized from getting hit by an oncoming eighteen wheeler. What I mean is this—there are times to step in and yell stop at the top of our lungs to make sure our kids don't walk into oncoming traffic. There are also times to let them run into the wall so that they learn not to do that again. Again, it requires Holy Spirit to help us discern those situations. We have all felt the pain of watching people we love or lead make devastating mistakes that had long-term consequences. I pray that in those situations we would have the courage to stand up and confront. I have also watched a generation that has been given way too much advice about situations that are only temporary learning experiences. This has caused many of them to feel smothered and pull away instead of feeling protected and drawing near.

## 6. *Discipleship Leads to Empowerment*

I am astounded at the way Jesus empowered people. It might be a better description to say that I am often frustrated and confronted by the way Jesus empowered people. If you have been around my ministry at all, then you know that empowerment is a core value. It is rare to go to a service that I am ministering in and not hear from one of the people I am discipling or at minimum see them ministering to people after service. I believe in empowerment, but Jesus clearly believed in it way more than I do. He was willing to take a man who had a legion of demons yesterday and send him out as an evangelist today (Mark 5:19)! That is what you call a one-step empowerment program. He sends out the disciples to do the work of the ministry and when they come back fighting over who is the greatest, He decides to send out seventy more. I'm going to be very honest here. If a few of my disciples were arguing in front of me about who was better at ministry, then I would probably have a very stern conversation with them and then possibly make them read a few books on humility before I let them minister again. I often struggle with the thought that I might be empowering a person too soon because of their immaturity, and yet Jesus barely got them to stop trying to call down fire from heaven to consume people while He was still sending them out as ministers.

Now please understand, I am not advocating for promoting people who have obvious character flaws into public ministry, especially not without confrontation and repentance, but if I sit with these Scriptures long enough then I have to admit that we are not doing the best job at empowering the next generation. We are usually waiting for some unde-termined point of maturity when we feel comfortable enough to let them lead. This is what was appalling to the church about Asbury. Shockingly, these Gen Z leaders were flawed and predom-inantly untrained, and yet still God chose them, and still their leaders empowered them.

> **These Gen Z leaders were flawed and predominantly untrained, and yet still God chose them, and still their leaders empowered them.**

I do not know what empow-erment needs to look like in your sphere of influence, whether it be your church, your ministry, your workplace, or your family, but I am convinced that discipleship always leads to empowerment. It is understandable that in the beginning, just like Jesus with the disciples, we would say, "You watch while I do." After a time, we will say, "Let's do this together." Eventually, we will be able to say, "You go do it, I'm going to watch you, and then we can reflect on how it went." One day we will say, "You can do it whether I am there or not."

I have practically laid this out in our ministry with those I dis-ciple. I meet with them one-on-one consistently for a period of time. As trust is built on both of our parts, I invite them to become more and more part of my world. As we develop a relationship in which there is enough trust for confrontation (this happens at different rates of time depending on the person and their history) then I begin to empower them. I refuse to empower someone I cannot confront. The more I see this person willing to engage in discipleship and to grow then I am able to more frequently and even more prominently empower them.

Let me make one important point. In my world, much empowerment often results in time in the pulpit, but this should not be the primary place of empowerment. From the beginning of your discipleship relationship, we can begin to empower those around us to pray for others, prophesy, minister to the sick, love our neighbors, and participate in Kingdom activity that every believer should engage in, even if they never hold a microphone in their entire lives. To be a disciple of Jesus does not mean leading a ministry or preaching a sermon, and we cannot confuse that point. We empower them to do the very things that Jesus gave authority to every believer to do. It is laid out clearly in Mark 16.

> And He said to them, "Go into all the world and preach the gospel to all creation. The one who has believed and has been baptized will be saved; but the one who has not believed will be condemned. These signs will accompany those who have believed: in My name they will cast out demons, they will speak with new tongues; they will pick up serpents, and if they drink any deadly poison, it will not harm them; they will lay hands on the sick, and they will recover" (**Mark 16:15-18 NASB**).

With this being our criteria, we can all empower the next generation and, more importantly, we all should be empowering the next generation. This is ultimately how we will see sustained revival—by discipling and empowering the next generation to do the same. We have to teach this generation how to give away what has been given to them. In an instant-gratification, it's-all-about-me world, there is much to gain as we all engage in the process of discipleship relationships that require humility and love.

## Notes

1. Simon Sinek, "How to Really Help Yourself," Facebook, April 8, 2021, https://www.facebook.com/simonsinek/videos/how-to-really-help-yourself/146244214091440.

2. Steven Robertson, *Aliens Among Us* (Houston, TX: Battle Ground Creative, 2022), 2.

3. Brené Brown, *Dare to Lead* (New York, NY: Random House, 2018), 48.

4. Robertson, *Aliens Among Us,* 8.

5. Kinnaman and Matlock, *Faith for Exiles,* 51.

# REFLECTION QUESTIONS

1. Have you personally experienced "discipleship" that was more like an employer/employee relationship? If so, what was the fruit in your life?

2. Who is discipling you currently, and whom can you disciple, if you are not already doing so?

3. How can you become a more Christlike mentor to a younger disciple?

4. How do you deal with confrontation? Do you avoid it? Do you have success or failure stories from the past?

5. How do you respond if someone confronts you?

6. Are you willing to empower the younger generation, as Holy Spirit leads, even if they seem immature to you?

*Chapter 11*

# BRIDGING THE GAP

One of the burning questions from the older generation is often, "Will they even listen to me?" or even weightier, "Do I have anything to offer?" What we have failed to realize is this generation doesn't need a sage; they don't even need you to be a Savior (that's what Jesus is for). They do, however, desperately need real parents. This is the first generation in history that is overwhelmingly mentored by their peers, and primarily online.[1] They have a broad network of YouTube celebrities and social media influencers to choose from. They do not lack access to knowledge; however, they have a huge deficit of real love. One thing that they cannot get from a screen is intentional, personal, genuine love.

For this chapter, I decided to reach out to a few Gen Z and ask them some questions. I wanted to do my best to bring a perspective outside the world you probably see on a daily basis. The reality is the older generation has valid concerns for the younger generation. We're worried that they want nothing to do with the church, we're concerned that they've lost a biblical worldview, and in so many ways we see them as a lost cause. I often wonder if what concerns me about the next generation is also concerning to the Christians who are in that generation. Perhaps if we could find some common ground, we wouldn't be so hesitant to approach them and work together for the challenges that the church is currently facing.

Following are the questions that were asked and a few of the responses. (Not every response was included.)

## WHAT HAS GOD SHOWN YOU SPECIFICALLY ABOUT YOUR GENERATION?

I see my generation going through a hype phase that eventually wears out due to their "Christian calling" not being their number one priority. ...There is a huge drive to build their own success and the Christian lifestyle doesn't always fit into this. ...I see a generation of leaders who need to be guided toward their purpose to walk out the fullness of their calling, but I don't see enough leaders who have gone before them stepping up to guide them.

**Jo Santana**

The Lord's highlighted my generation's measure of fierceness and desperation. Desperate to find a belief that holds value; longing to become passionate for something. Some, unfortunately, find their heart to beat with the rhythm of the world, but I believe that there's a greater number than we realize who have found their heart to beat in alignment with the Father's. Whether it be for the world or for the Kingdom, I've found my generation to be one that's desperate to be fiercely set ablaze for something.

**Reese Mikrut**

That He is raising up a generation of disciples again (Luke 10:23-24). He called the unqualified ones from the human perspective, the ones without a theology degree, the fishermen. Now he is calling them again, Gen Z. The first thing the disciples did after Jesus called them was immediately drop everything, which means that He is calling but each one of us has to make a personal decision to drop everything to follow Him. ...After leaving everything behind they were trained and equipped, and they were put under the authority of Jesus. I feel like Jesus is also calling Gen Z to position themselves under the authority of Christ and of the ones He has given authority on earth. That way they were able to walk in His authority and carry revival with the coming of the Holy Spirit. ...I also believe that the areas the Lord is highlighting in this season are the ones the enemy tries to attack the most. If the statistics say my generation is the most depressed one, I believe that the Lord says they are a generation of joy. If the numbers say we are the most anxious generation, I believe the Lord says we are a generation of peace. If people call us the most atheist generation, I believe that the Lord calls us the most hungry generation for Him.

**Giulia Mynssen**

# WHAT DO YOU SEE AS THE GREATEST CHALLENGE FACING YOUR GENERATION?

The lack of prioritizing emotional and spiritual health along with a lack of urgency in promoting the Kingdom of God while carrying holiness, integrity, and Christlike character.

**Jo Santana**

Feeling the need to have our words align with both society's values as well as with those that are biblical. We cater to all truths in the name of care and respect for our neighbor, not realizing that when we disregard the truth, we're just neglecting the reality of people's eternity. ...The greatest challenge facing this generation is choosing to completely place down our fear of man, to grasp strongly our fear of God. Choosing whether or not we'll lay down our whole selves— even our reputation—solely for the advancement of the Gospel.

**Reese Mikrut**

# HOW IMPORTANT IS THE BIBLE IN YOUR DAILY WALK WITH CHRIST?

When Moses led the nation of Israel into the wilderness toward the Promised Land, there was a daily portion of manna that sustained them (Exodus 16). I see the word of God in the same way. There is a new portion of sustenance from Heaven that I receive daily when I encounter the Lord through His Word. It has become more of a necessity rather than a good idea.

**Jo Santana**

The Bible is the written word of God (*logos*), so it's impossible to say we fully know Him if we don't know the Bible. If I want to access deeper levels of intimacy with Him, I need to know what He says, what are His promises to me, and how to live by His commandments. I consider the Bible the written manual to life, the foundation of all my decisions, and the filter I use to see the world. For me, the Bible is part of the *daily* food I need to consume to feed my spirit.

**Giulia Mynssen**

> **There is a new portion of sustenance from Heaven that I receive daily when I encounter the Lord through His Word. It has become more of a necessity rather than a good idea.**

## DO YOU CONSIDER YOURSELF TO HAVE A "BIBLICAL WORLDVIEW"? WHY OR WHY NOT?

Yes. I believe the Bible is the framework from which I view reality and make sense of life and the world. My beliefs about what is wrong and what is right, what is ethical and what is unethical come from the Bible and not from men. If at any point in my life, I need to decide between something that someone said or the Bible, the Bible is my choice because I believe that the Lord doesn't operate in ways that compete with or go against the Bible.

**Giulia Mynssen**

Yes. I credit my worldview partially to my upbringing, and the other half of reasoning for my biblical worldview I credit to the history and relationship I have been building with the Lord over the last couple of years. As a result of this relationship my opinions, desires, beliefs, and perspectives have all been influenced by that relationship. I have the worldview I have because of who I love.

**Jo Santana**

I do. If I live my life saying that Jesus is worthy of it all, "all" must include my every opinion, outlook, and view. And if Jesus, the Man I consider worthy of everything, is the word made flesh, my worldview must be biblical. He is the only One worthy, and He has captivated my every opinion.

**Reese Mikrut**

## HOW RECEPTIVE ARE YOU TO BEING DISCIPLED? WHAT DOES THAT LOOK LIKE FOR YOU?

I didn't know I needed to be discipled before being discipled. Today with the understanding of discipleship being life-on-life, I find myself in a place where I wish I knew more people who were being discipled (in the biblical perspective) directly by a spiritual mother or father. Discipleship is sacrifice on both ends. You choose to have this person as family. Because of your commitment to the calling of God in your life, you choose to be discipled and to disciple. Discipleship looks like living a transparent life with your discipler and trusting, serving, honoring, loving, and investing into God's calling over your life while you are being invested into by your disciple.

**Jo Santana**

There was a time in my life when I'd say I was 0 percent receptive, but now I'd say that I'm very receptive to being discipled. I had to repent for an immense amount of pride and ask Holy Spirit for a heart of humility. For me, being discipled looks like having a true desperation to learn and grow and learning how to embrace guidance and correction. But alongside this desperation has been this immense value for vulnerability. Letting trusted leaders into the messiest places of my heart and life; not only being honest with them about those spaces but giving them permission to see them in their depths. I had to lay down my desire for everything in my life to look perfectly pretty from the outside, and pick up a desperation for things to not be in shambles anymore on the inside—and that took opening up fully about all of my mess. We must uncover, in all vulnerability, our broken pieces if we ever want help being mended. How beautiful it is to have leaders in step with Holy Spirit, shepherding you to where the Lord has you going.

**Reese Mikrut**

Looking at some verses like Hebrews 13:17 and Romans 13:1-2 I have not found one Scripture in the Bible that says that putting yourself under authority and being a disciple causes you harm—the opposite actually, that doing it with groaning brings no advantage to us. I have found that discipleship is a blessing and a gift from the Lord. That people can see more than what I see, that putting yourself in a position of being discipled brings pruning, and pruning is an invitation to growth. So if there are people who see more in me than even myself, I think my posture is to rip my chest open and work together with them if that means being uncomfortable and painful or not. That being said, discipleship for me is doing life together. In my opinion it's putting yourself in a position of vulnerability, obedience, and being teachable. At times it means trusting blindly the one who is leading. The disciples most of the time had no clue what Jesus was talking about or

> **How beautiful it is to have leaders in step with Holy Spirit, shepherding you to where the Lord has you going.**

at least the length of it, but they daily made the decision of putting themselves under His authority.

**Giulia Mynssen**

## WHAT DO YOU WISH THE OLDER GENERATION KNEW ABOUT YOUR GENERATION?

The methods have changed but the goal is the same. We need a healthy dynamic between the old and the young, sons and fathers. I always think about Joel 2:28. While the younger generation prophesies and takes steps of action, the older generation needs to be there giving vision and imparting what the Lord is saying. Besides that, in a more practical term, the years of wisdom and experience that the older generation has can only serve to benefit my generation.

**Jo Santana**

We want spiritual moms and dads, disciplers, and mentors who are willing to guide us in the process of life. We appreciate everything that has been done; we honor the ones who paid a high price for us to have access to what we have today. Don't just give us the tools and steps to have a good life; we want you to do it with us and not just our Christian lives. We don't believe Christianity can be separated from our work, our relationships, and the rest of our lives.

**Giulia Mynssen**

## WHAT IS YOUR RELATIONSHIP WITH THE CHURCH AND HOW IMPORTANT DO YOU THINK IT IS TO YOUR WALK WITH CHRIST?

I love the church, and it's very important to my walk with Christ. I think it's an easy place to take for granted, but the bride giving their whole self to love, adore, and await the Bridegroom is something I've come to value and something I never want to not be apart from. I love the house of the Lord.

**Reese Mikrut**

Church is the body of Christ on earth. If you don't love the bride, there is no way for you to love the groom; they are one. I love being part of the church and serving it. It's a place where in unity we can worship God and give Him our gratitude in different ways. Even though the church is not limited to a building, its manifested inside of one.

**Giulia Mynssen**

The church cannot be washed down to be seen as a good organization for me and for society. The church is a part of the Kingdom of God that acts to advance and promote (in both a corporate and individual manner) the reality of Heaven on earth. The church is not there to massage my ego or to promote my name, but it is there as a "base" to equip the saints to live out the great commission. The church is what Jesus built the foundation for in the three and a half years of ministry He had on earth. For us to neglect the church is for us to be ignorant of what Jesus initiated and the apostles built.

**Jo Santana**

## WHEN YOU HEAR THE TERM "MULTI-GENERATIONAL REVIVAL" WHAT DO YOU THINK OF?

Spiritual parents and kids coming together with no agenda to seek the Lord. Gen Z is ahead but is sustained by the older generation. I think of hundreds of generations that have built the foundation through prayer years ago coming together with the maturity, wisdom, and experience of the present leaders and the hunger, boldness, and love of the younger ones culminating in revival.

**Giulia Mynssen**

I think of two passages of Scripture. Joel 2:28 because we see all the generations actively involved. Second, I think of Acts 16:31-34 because revival culminates in family being restored and the whole family being involved in what God is doing, not just one specific generation.

**Jo Santana**

I think of every age coming together in unity, bowing low before the King. I see leaders longing for their ceilings to be the next person's floor. The ones being led longing to learn from the ones who've gone before them. I see people not magnifying anyone's age, but rather having eyes to see each one's anointing. A magnitude of people—young and old, children and parents—running together after the prize. I hear hearts beating in sync—a rhythm not determined by age, but rather by a unified love for One.

**Reese Mikrut**

# RECOUNT FOR US A MIRACLE YOU'VE SEEN DONE IN OR THROUGH SOMEONE (INCLUDING YOURSELF) IN YOUR GENERATION.

In 2019, I was translating at a church conference in Southern Brazil. After three intense days of ministry, the senior pastor asked me to close the conference. Immediately, I felt the Lord wanting to bring healing into the room. As I opened my mouth to pray, I felt the Holy Spirit saying that He would touch people with healing; there would be no need for the laying on of hands. As I prayed that over the church the place erupted in shouts of praise, of shock, and of marvel. I then asked for all who had been healed to lift up their hands and dozens responded. The next day the regional pastors of the area pulled me into a car without any explanation. They started playing an audio message in which a middle-aged woman explained that the night before she attended the conference, she was covering every area of her body from her neck to her feet due to tumors that were spread all over her body. Her voice began to crack as she expressed the moment when a young man prayed and she felt every single tumor imploding and disappearing without anyone laying hands on her. The following day she went on to find out she was tumor free and cancer free!

**Jo Santana**

For me, the biggest miracle this generation has experienced is inside of themselves. Not the healing of a temporary body, but the transformation of something eternal, our own lives being transformed. It is amazing to see miracles and healing happening in the natural, but in the Bible when there was a healing or a miracle the name of Jesus was glorified and people started following Him. The word Jesus used for healing was *sozo*, which means complete healing, not only the healing of your physical body but also the healing of your emotions and what is inside of you, what cannot be seen. The end is not the miracle, but Jesus being glorified and lives being forever changed. In a generation that loves the self, one of the biggest miracles is people choosing Jesus over themselves. In a generation that has access to a lot of information through technology, a miracle is people choosing to humble themselves and acknowledge that they know nothing apart from Jesus.

**Giulia Mynssen**

## INCLUDE ANYTHING YOU FEEL NEEDS TO BE SAID ABOUT GEN Z, MULTI-GENERATIONAL REVIVAL, AND WHAT GOD IS DOING NOW.

There is a window of opportunity for my generation to partner with the older generation in embracing true discipleship as we walk through such unique times. I see Gen Z as an underdog generation that has the potential to see the Lord do things we haven't heard, dreamed, or imagined yet. As long as I have breath in my lungs I will not let my generation casually step into lukewarm Christianity.

**Jo Santana**

**In a generation that has access to a lot of information through technology, a miracle is people choosing to humble themselves and acknowledge that they know nothing apart from Jesus.**

He is raising up a younger generation with hungry hearts but not necessarily mature ones. In that, there is an opportunity for the older generation to disciple and guide the younger ones, partnering with what the Lord is doing in their lives. We are hungry and we will do whatever it takes to see His face, but we need key elements that you carry. I believe in a generation that burns for the Lord with all that they are—I believe in a generation that will see revival.

**Giulia Mynssen**

The more I find myself in intentional conversations with the believers in Gen Z, the more I realize we're not that different after all. Oh sure, I don't like the majority of the music they listen to, and I'm still not sure why girls are wearing sneakers with dresses and calling it dressed up, but ultimately they love Jesus, the church, and their generation. We might not use the same jargon or understand how they can spend hours on their cell phones; however, there is a Bartimaeus generation that has a remnant of on-fire believers who want to see revival in their schools, churches, cities, and nations. There may be perceived "generational gaps," but there is undoubtedly one Spirit who lives in us. It is time we set aside the differences for the Kingdom purpose of Jesus exalted.

Note

1.  Robertson, *Aliens Among Us,* 134.

# REFLECTION QUESTIONS

1. As you read these answers, how well did you feel you relate to these young people?

2. Do you find yourself agreeing with these young perspectives or differing from them?

3. If you are older than Gen Z, can you see your generation participating with these young people to further the Kingdom?

4. What is the most encouraging thing to hear from these young people?

5. What area do you feel most called to take an active role in, after hearing their thoughts?

6. Are there any agendas you might hold for Gen Z that you need to let go of and simply seek Jesus' Presence together?

# CONCLUSION

The Bartimaeus generation is rising up.

Bartimaeus was discredited and unlikely and yet he stands out in the Gospels as one of great faith. He rose above adversity and locked eyes with Jesus. His tenacity and courage led to a miracle. As this generation lays aside all of the labels put on them, they have locked eyes with Jesus, and God is showing up for them. Jesus is proverbially stopping for this generation just as He did for Bartimaeus. He is calling them.

This will be the generation that hosts revival.

The time is absolutely now. It is the time for revival. God is looking for a people who will believe Him and partner with what He is doing in the earth. I can't help but ask myself and you the questions: Are we all in? Are we really ready for revival to come?

Perhaps this revival isn't happening how we thought. It surely doesn't look like we thought it would, but here we are. Are we all in no matter what it looks like? If we are, then am I willing to embrace what God is doing now and how He is doing it. It is time we let go of our preconceived ideas of what this revival is supposed to look like and instead fully commit to this next move of God. No matter the cost, let's go all in.

What if the piece we've been missing truly is inside this generation that has been considered the least likely? I will believe the report of the Lord. I will believe what He said about them.

So now the charge is to you and me! Will we step up as a mother or father for this generation? Take one of these young fire starters and disciple them in the ways of following Jesus. Just like in roller derby, we need all hands on deck. We need the young and the old to step out together to bring in the harvest that is waiting for us. We are on the precipice of revival, the field is ripe for harvest, and the laborers are waiting to be sent.

There is a generation that has been put on the sidelines, but they are more than ready to jump into the game. They are simply waiting for mothers and fathers to stand beside them and give them the charge to "Go!"

I cannot promise you that it will be easy. In fact, I can guarantee you that it will be messy at times. Partnering with God to transform a nation is not for the faint of heart. Rescuing a generation from a godless culture is for the warriors. It is for the determined. It is for those who refuse to be denied. Will you join me?

I want to end this book with a challenge for you. Maybe you don't have a big ministry or a big church with thousands of young people you influence weekly, but do you have just one? I challenge you to ask God for just one or two names of someone in the younger generation you can take under your wing and disciple. You do not need as much as you think you do. God has put inside of you all that you need to disciple them. You do not have to go buy a pair of Nike Air Force Ones (or any cool shoes) and you do not have to know what the most recent song to go viral is.

> **Partnering with God to transform a nation is not for the faint of heart. Rescuing a generation from a godless culture is for the warriors.**

All you need is to know Jesus and have a heart to see these young ones follow Jesus. Set aside time and see this as the necessity that it is to revival.

Take those one or two young people and make a commitment to invest your time into them. Prioritize it on your calendar. Let them know that you are committed to seeing them reach their full potential in Christ. Pray for them. Then, be a parent. Love them like you would love your own. Lead them and guide them in the ways of Jesus. Have copious amounts of fun and laughter. Make sure you're available for the good times and the bad. Pray and pray and pray some more with them, over them, and for them. Trust God to help you as you disciple them into a mature follower of Jesus who walks in His character and power.

I believe in you.

Let's see the Bartimaeus generation arise.

# ABOUT JESSIKA TATE

**Jessika Tate** is an international speaker, missionary, author, and unashamed coffee lover who has been traveling the world preaching the Gospel for over fifteen years in some of the darkest places on earth. She is the founder of Yielded Ministries, a nonprofit organization that focuses on training the body of Christ to yield fully to Him while providing aid and advocacy for vulnerable communities. In addition to Yielded, she is the leader of Apostello Movement, which uses Bible studies, retreats, and trainings to equip the next generation of female church leaders. She currently resides in Franklin, Tennessee.

**www.yieldedministries.com**

**www.apostellomovement.com**

From
# Jessi Green

## Will you be baptized? Or swept away?

Today, many Christians are disillusioned by the empty promises of dry religion. They long for an authentic, biblical transformation in their lives, but have yet to encounter a faith that works.

Jessi Green has witnessed the Holy Spirit transform the lives of thousands of hungry souls who were willing to abandon dead faith and seek out true revival.

In *Saturate*, revivalist and evangelist, Jessi Green offers a prophetic forecast of the coming flood of the Holy Spirit, helping you break free of dry religion and immerse yourself in the saturating presence of God.

*Saturate* was birthed by a prophetic vision where Jessi saw seven waves of judgment, deliverance, and power crash over the nation. How you respond to this tsunami will determine your eternal destiny!

Don't settle for lifeless, status quo religion. Will you be baptized in this prophetic outpouring, or be swept away by the Holy flood?

## Purchase your copy wherever books are sold

From
# Jennifer A. Miskov

## Fasting is about feasting on more of God!

When many hear the word *fasting*, they immediately think of what they have to give up.

But what if fasting is more about *gaining* God than giving up?

What if fasting is a sacred doorway into fresh encounters with the all-consuming fire of God?

Author and revival historian, Jennifer A. Miskov, has tapped into an ancient pathway to divine encounter. She has given her life to studying how the great pioneers of revival experienced dynamic moves of the Holy Spirit, both in their personal lives and in the corporate church.

One of the key common denominators is fasting. Historically, fasting was never a formula for holiness or a means to manipulate God. In fact, in revival history, "the fasting ones" were actually "the feasting ones"—those who single-mindedly aligned themselves with what heaven wanted to release into the earth.

Featuring easy-to-follow fasting exercises, Scripture meditations, reflection questions, activations, and special chapters by Randy Clark and Lou Engle, *Fasting for Fire* will stir you to pursue the presence of God with more passion and zeal than ever before!

## Purchase your copy wherever books are sold

From
# Joanne Moody

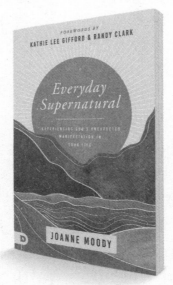

**Experience Miracles Wherever You Go... even in unexpected places!**

Is your heart crying out for more? Do you long to experience the supernatural? Do you want to live a life marked by Kingdom adventure? Then join Joanne Moody for a life-changing faith journey in *Everyday Supernatural*!

Since experiencing her own life-changing supernatural healing, Joanne Moody has made it her mission to give away the love and miracles of Jesus everywhere she goes. She believes this is the power and privilege of every believer!

In *Everyday Supernatural*, Joanne Moody serves up a spiritual feast of captivating testimonies, practical teaching, and powerful activations. You will walk away emboldened with the knowledge that God is intent on using everyday people to perform His miracles and reveal His Son to the world!

Jesus wants to work through *you* to supernaturally touch the people around you. From your local grocery store to your workplace, from your school to your favorite coffee shop, it's time to begin releasing miracles everywhere you go!

## Purchase your copy wherever books are sold

# YOUR
# *Prophetic*
# C O M M U N I T Y

Sign up for a **FREE** subscription to the Destiny Image digital magazine and get awesome content delivered directly to your inbox!

### destinyimage.com/signup

## Sign up for Cutting-Edge Messages that Supernaturally Empower You

• Gain valuable insights and guidance based on biblical principles
• Deepen your faith and understanding of God's plan for your life
• Receive regular updates and prophetic messages
• Connect with a community of believers who share your values and beliefs

## Experience Fresh Video Content that Reveals Your Prophetic Inheritance

• Receive prophetic messages and insights
• Connect with a powerful tool for spiritual growth and development
• Stay connected and inspired on your faith journey

## Listen to Powerful Podcasts that Propel You into God's Presence Every Day

• Deepen your understanding of God's prophetic assignment
• Experience God's revival power throughout your day
• Learn how to grow spiritually in your walk with God

# In the Right Hands, This Book Will Change Lives!

Most of the people who need this message will not be looking for this book. To change their lives, you need to **put a copy of this book in their hands.**

Our ministry is constantly seeking methods to find the people who need this anointed message to change their lives. **Will you help us reach these people?**

**Extend this ministry by sowing three, five, ten, or *even more* books today and change people's lives for the better!** Your generosity will be part of catalyzing the Great Awakening that many have been prophesying and praying for.